BEING THE MOUNTAIN
PRODUCTORA

PRODUCTORA's practice is both preternaturally mature and distinctly contemporary. Carlos Bedoya, Wonne Ickx, Victor Jamie, and Abel Perles, the firm's four partners, each contribute to this practice by and through different perspectives, often working from a distance. Since forming in 2006, they have set their objectives extremely high, continually defining a project of precise, legible, expertly crafted architecture that creates compelling relationships between geometry, material, and occupant.

At the same time, their work deeply engages its contexts, current and past. Their temporary Pavilion on the Zocalo, winner of the 2016 Mies Crown Hall Americas Prize (MCHAP) for Emerging Practice, intelligently brought together historical and material narratives to "make explicit the contested history of an important civic space in Mexico City," as jury chair Stan Allen wrote of the project. The Teopanzolco Cultural Center, realized in Cuernavaca in 2017 with Isaac Broid and a finalist for the 2018 Americas Prize, forges an extremely relevant, edifying interaction between an archaeological site and today's public realm. Crucially, this work also happens through more than building: LIGA, the cultural space that PRODUCTORA founded in 2011 with the curator Ruth Estévez, has become a locus for architectural conversations in Mexico City. Along with their teaching, these projects are a clear statement of the breadth of the practice's interests and collaborative methods, and an example of the roles architects can have in shaping architecture and its ideas more widely.

This book is a direct result of the investigations PRODUCTORA undertook as MCHAP prizewinners. Housed in the Illinois Institute of Technology (IIT) College of Architecture, the Mies Crown Hall Americas Prize recognizes excellence in architecture in the Americas and includes two awards: the Americas Prize, given to the best building realized in North or South America in the previous two years, and the Prize for Emerging Practice, given to the best building completed during the same period by a firm in its first ten years of operation. The 2016 jury included Allen, Ila Berman, Jean Pierre Crousse, Florencia Rodriguez, and Wiel Arets, who initiated MCHAP in 2012, during his deanship of the College of Architecture; they selected Pavilion on the Zocalo as the Emerging Practice winner from over one hundred nominated works. As authors of the winning project, the partners of PRODUCTORA were invited to teach at IIT and given $25,000 toward research and a publication. In this sense, the book you are holding—and the conversations it has made and will make possible—is the award.

MCHAP's focus on the Americas and its location within the academy are key aspects of the prize. The countries of the Americas have diverse but intertwining histories; their present is one of challenging realities and extreme potential, a condition in which architecture has played an integral role. The Americas offer specific evidence of how architectural knowledge is now moving in new directions and along underused paths, opening up exciting possibilities for addressing contemporary issues. We believe that a school of architecture is a natural place for this awareness to be absorbed. With that in mind, MCHAP's interest has always been in not what architecture is, but what it does—instructive cases of architectural excellence contributing to the character of communities on the ground. It is perhaps not a surprise, then, that PRODUCTORA has taken up something so fundamental as the ground itself in this book. As they write, flying frequently between Chicago and Mexico City put topographical differences front of mind for the firm, providing a new lens for reflecting on their previous work and material for the studios they taught at IIT in the fall of 2017 and the spring of 2018.

We are grateful to have been enriched by this exchange and by PRODUCTORA's presence on the IIT faculty in S. R. Crown Hall, MCHAP's home base, which also has lessons to offer here. While at first Crown Hall might read as a lantern floating above the midwestern plains, through PRODUCTORA's research, we might recast its cascading travertine steps as a topographical exploration, one that introduces variety and choreographs connections. Its studios are also both upstairs and downstairs, the latter embedded, like the building itself, in the ground. Situated above, at, and below grade during their time in Chicago, PRODUCTORA reminds us of the richness we can find when we look at modernism again from where we are now.

Dirk Denison, FAIA
Director, Mies Crown Hall Americas Prize
Professor, College of Architecture, IIT

This book is an outcome of two studios we taught at the College of Architecture at Illinois Institute of Technology (IIT) in Chicago in 2017 and 2018, whose line of research continued in a symposium and exhibition held at S. R. Crown Hall in November 2018.

PRODUCTORA received the Mies Crown Hall Americas Prize for Emerging Practice in 2016 for our project Pavilion on the Zocalo, and as part of the award, we were invited to teach a so-called "cloud studio" at IIT. Triggered by the stark contrast between the geographical conditions in Mexico and the vast horizontal plains of Illinois, all too apparent in our frequent trips back and forth, we conceived both studios to examine the relationship between architecture and topography. The first studio, in fall 2017, was titled "Being the Mountain" and investigated hillside housing as a central theme. The title was taken from Ricardo Legorreta's

A superposition of generic suburban plan layouts and pronounced topographies. Craig Ellwood, architect. Marvin Rand, photographer. Smith House, Los Angeles, 1958.

description of the Camino Real hotel in Ixtapa (1981), a resort spread across an ocean-facing slope of the Sierra Madre. The project constitutes a powerful example of a building that engages with topography without falling into nostalgic placemaking or the organic mimicking of natural contours. The second studio, in fall 2018, was entitled "Elevated Surface Depressed," after a 1982 work by the artist Michael Heizer. Heizer placed natural objects above, on top of, or within a geometric plinth, questioning the relation between human-made and natural objects and between natural and artificial landscapes. Students in the studio were asked to develop an underground or elevated building on a flat site in Chicago's Loop.

Expanding on the studios, this book focuses on what may be one of the most evident themes in architecture: the fact that a building—one way or another—has to come down and touch the ground. It might be the absolute obviousness of this fact that makes it an infrequently discussed topic, but to consider it head on contributes fresh perspective on the postwar reaction against a heroic modernism and its ideals of unification, standardization, and universalism. Modern architecture often had a cumbersome relationship with the land it occupied: spurred by a plan-driven design logic and the industrialization of the building process, uneven landscapes were regularly scraped flat or mediated by plinths, allowing the architect an untarnished

Le Corbusier uses pilotis to mediate the irregularities of the terrain. La Tourette, Éveux, France, 1960.

datum of clean orthogonality. In the first of his five points, Le Corbusier declared that buildings had to be removed from "the dampness of the soil" by means of pilotis. His position did more than reflect a constructive-technical logic, however; it also had a profound cultural significance. For Le Corbusier, architecture would "no longer be an archaic entity, heavily rooted into the soil by deep foundations, built 'firm and strong,' the object of devotion on which the cult of the family and the race has so long been concentrated."[1] Disconnecting the buildings from the ground was a formal expression of an explicit ideological stance. Arguably, Ludwig Mies van der Rohe's Farnsworth House constitutes an iconic representation of the same modern position. While most of Mies's buildings are thoroughly anchored to the ground by foundation slabs, plinths, or basement levels, this small dwelling was elevated five feet (1.5 meters) above grade to anticipate the regular overflowing of the adjacent Fox River. The outcome was a building that hovers weightlessly over a grassy meadow. Although the reasoning behind the Farnsworth House was absolutely pragmatic and topological, it can be read as a metaphor for the rupture with the "foundations" declared by Le Corbusier.

Modern architects had insinuated the need for a more site-specific approach since the first meetings of the Congrès internationaux d'architecture moderne (CIAM), but it was not until the middle of the twentieth century that ideas about history, context, territory, and finally topography came fully to the foreground. The export of modern architecture to peripheral places like Mexico, Brazil, and California played a crucial role in this process. In these places, dramatic topographical conditions became a perfect remedy for the glooming fatigue of a modern architecture that was being flattened out more and more as a suburban lifestyle commodity. The integration of buildings into the landscape was a decisive—yet rarely explored—strategy to counter the commodification of architecture in the second half of the twentieth century.

Le Corbusier. Sketch from *Précisions sur un état présent de l'architecture et de l'urbanisme* (Paris, 1930).

We have invited three outside contributors to further examine the topic from particular vantage points. Véronique Patteeuw looks at the writing of Kenneth Frampton, who rejected a placeless, scenographic architecture in favor of an approach exemplified by the Greek architect Dimitris Pikionis, the Portuguese architect Álvaro Siza, and the Mexican architect Luis Barragán, among others. Frank Escher considers the role of earth conditions in the development of modern architecture in California, exploring the work of Frank Lloyd Wright, R. M. Schindler, and John Lautner. Lastly, Jesús Vassallo reads the Royal Collections Museum in Madrid, by Mansilla + Tuñón, as a giant retention wall withholding different time scales of history and geology. Invoking Robert Smithson, Vassallo questions how we might understand architecture's role in shaping the land now that the greatest force of geological transformation is in fact human activity. The November 2018 exhibition and symposium provided an opportunity to gather all three authors in Chicago; after a closed working session at the Graham Foundation, they presented their contributions at Crown Hall, followed by a roundtable discussion.

A last component of this book includes a series of projects by PRODUCTORA chosen retrospectively to illustrate topography as an elementary force that has stimulated our architectural proposals. Developed in very diverse regions of Mexico—the sandy

Landscape and topography integrated into postwar city planning. Cesar Pelli. Proposal for Sunset Mountain Park, Santa Monica, California, 1966.

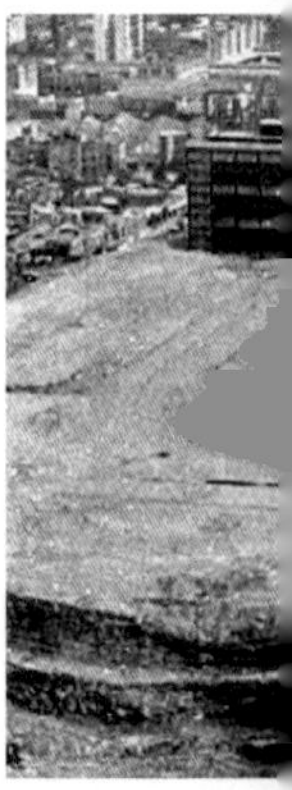

beaches of Quintana Roo, the hard basalt formations of Chihuahua—our work has been very much informed by the topographical and geological conditions of the sites where we intervene. From our earlier projects, like the proposals for Chanchan and the LIMAC museum, both in Peru, or the Tsunami Memorial Site, in Oslo, to more recently built work, our architecture frequently reveals a strong dialogue with the ground surface; sometimes projects are developed in explicit opposition to the landscape, while in other cases they enhance or echo the natural surroundings. In the proposals for the House in Ginigala, Sri Lanka, or the Blas House, in Valle de Bravo, the sloped topography becomes the central narrative around which the architectural idea is structured. The House in Chihuahua or the Teopanzolco Cultural Center are examples of how the existing context is integrated into the architecture, illustrating the idea of architecture as constructed ground. Topography, a word that brings together *topos* (place) and *graphein* (write), means literally the *writing of place*, and is therefore not only about the registration of surface relief, but about the writing—the construction—of the landscape as well.

Our fascination with earthworks and the land art movement of the 1970s might have played a crucial role in these architectural explorations. Powerful works like Heizer's *Double Negative*, Richard Serra's *Shift*, or Isamu Noguchi's proposed *Sculpture to Be Seen from Mars* (originally tilted *Monument to Man*) always appealed strongly to us. Reference images included in books on these artists—frequently pre-modern architecture from faraway places—came to inform our practice in turn, spurring our fascination with the monolithic churches in Lalibela, Ethiopia, Indian stepwells, Egyptian hypostyle halls, underground villages in China, and many other rarities. Inspired by these works of architectural archaeology and land art, along with the often impressive natural landscapes or historic settings in which our projects are embedded, we

Above and left: The never-finished El Helicoide was intended as a spiraling drive-in mall complementing the dramatic topography of Caracas. Pedro Neuberger, Dirk Bornhorst, and Jorge Romero Gutiérrez. 1956–61.

elaborated our own personal repertoire more or less consciously, with a specific attention to the geography of the region and the topographical singularities of the terrain. In this sense, our buildings are there to re-write and to give meaning to the context that surrounds them.

By the mid-twentieth century, the flatlands of San Juan, Puerto Rico, were already densely populated; urban planners turned to the surrounding hills to accommodate new housing infrastructure. Moshe Safdie. Model of Habitat Puerto Rico, 1971.

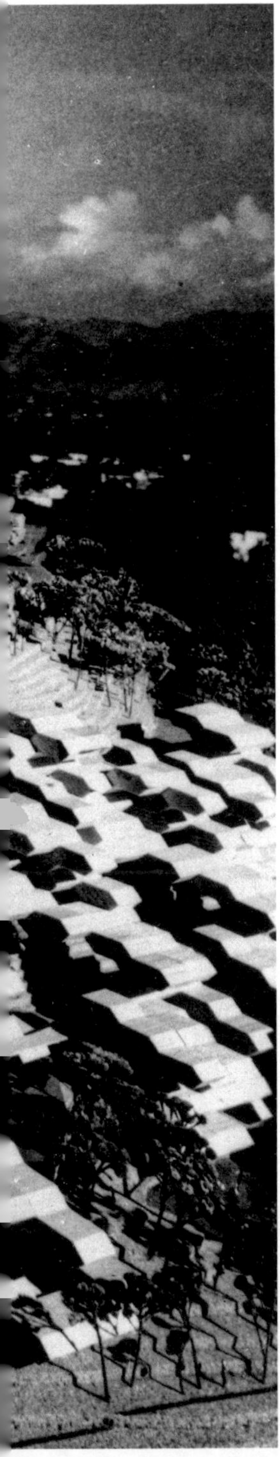

An unrealized proposal for a vast earthwork sculpture by Isamu Noguchi. Noguchi scaled the pyramidal nose to span one mile. *Sculpture to Be Seen from Mars* (also known as *Monument to Man*), 1947.

1 Le Corbusier, *Towards a New Architecture* (1931; repr., London: John Rodker, 1960), 237, 263.

> "The new design would not be a tower; it would not be a form on the mountain but *be* the mountain, with rooms terraced down the slope. It wouldn't fight with nature but blend with the topography."[1]

In 1981, the architect Ricardo Legorreta and his firm finished the construction of the Camino Real in Ixtapa, an impressive holiday resort draped over an ocean-facing slope of the Sierra Madre, on the Pacific coast of Mexico. The hotel was key in the development of Ixtapa, a tourist destination north of Acapulco that the Mexican government began promoting in the late sixties. By the time of this commission, Legorreta had become famous for his remarkable hotel designs, especially the Camino Real in Mexico City, built to host visitors to the 1968 Olympic Games. Heavily influenced by the hyper-rationalist José Villagrán, Legorreta's early work had mainly consisted of highly functional and cost-effective commercial projects, such as medical

A holiday resort draped over an ocean-facing slope of the Sierra Madre. Postcard from the Hotel Camino Real, Ixtapa, Mexico (1981), date unknown. Ricardo Legorreta, architect.

laboratories, car manufacturing plants, schools, and corporate offices. For the high-profile Mexico City project, the young Legorreta—then thirty-six years old—surrounded himself with an amazing group of designers and artists including Luis Barragán, Mathias Goeritz, Alexander Calder, Anni Albers, Pedro Friedeberg, and Rufino Tamayo. The encounter with artistic talent of such caliber defined a turning point in his career, infusing Legorreta's functionalist mindset with a desire for emotion and color and a deep interest in the roots of Mexican culture.

While the Camino Real in Mexico City played a crucial role in Legorreta's switch to what became a highly exportable "regionalist" style, it was also the first project in which he could test a horizontal hotel layout. Mid-century international hotels were typically large tower-and-plinth structures, combining a horizontal distribution of amenities and public programs in the base with an effective vertical circulation for both visitors and staff in the tower. However, to meet demanding deadlines that would ensure that the hotel would open in time for the Games, Legorreta was forced to explore different means of construction and circulation, and chose a low-rise scheme. Wide and well-lit hallways would take visitors to their rooms horizontally, multiplying the distance covered but adding a pleasant architectural quality to the experience. As a critic writing for *Architectural Forum* reported, "Guests have to do a lot of walking. Brockman [the owner of the hotel chain] briskly remarks that 'If the guests don't like to walk, they can always go to another hotel.'"[2] Legorreta relates this idea to a different interpretation of monumentality. Generally seen as a quality related to height or mass, for him, monumentality "was also in the horizon." "I think that that was a discovery—not just mine, but something that many people started to understand—that the horizon-

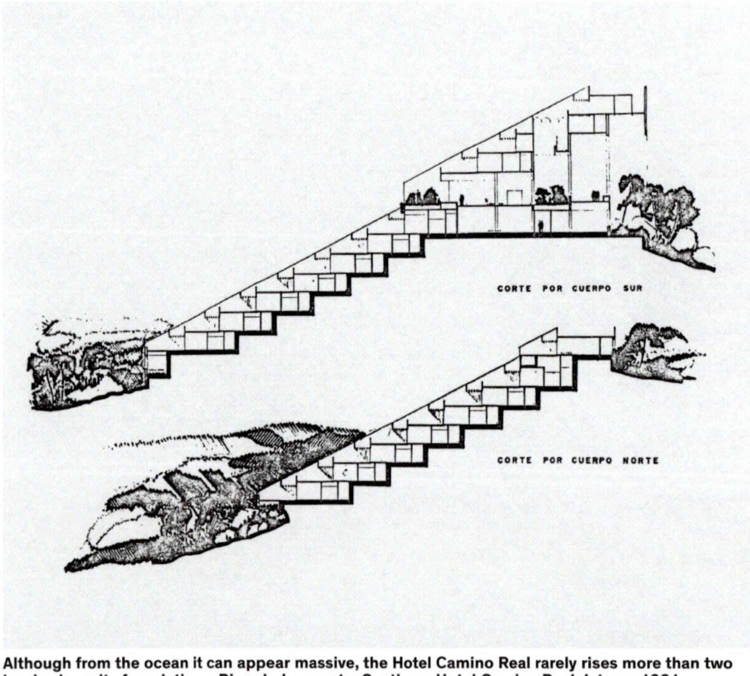

Although from the ocean it can appear massive, the Hotel Camino Real rarely rises more than two levels above its foundations. Ricardo Legorreta. Sections, Hotel Camino Real, Ixtapa, 1981.

A brochure promoting the 1950s Las Brisas hotel in Acapulco, Mexico, date unknown.

tality is very important and that is deduced from the pleasure of walking, which we had forgotten. The radical change that the elevators brought along, had changed architecture," he explained in a 2013 interview.[3]

Legorreta repeated this horizontal approach in 1975 at the Camino Real hotel in Cancun, but in Ixtapa, the hotel operator initially asked him for a rather conventional layout: a tower with gardens, restaurants, and pools at ground level. Nevertheless, at the same time, the client also longed for an atmosphere like that of the acclaimed Las Brisas hotel in Acapulco, a 1950s resort that covered an entire hill with pink-and-white bungalows and plunge pools. Such a scattered and loose organization—"designed by a sailor, not an architect," Legorreta mocked[4]—would be completely beyond the project's budget, according to the architect and his advisors. But if the client could acquire a different piece of land, Legorreta assured, he could generate a hotel that would have "the way of life of Las Brisas" within the established budget.[5] The client purchased a different piece of land with prominent topography and a private beach, and the project went ahead.

Just like in Las Brisas, the topography of the site defined the identity of the resort: it was realized as an extended volume enveloping the surface of a hill sloped toward the beach. Rooms are stacked one on top of the other, following the same inclination as the underlying topography—a fairly straightforward solution. Although from the ocean it can appear massive, with ten stories or more, the building rarely rises more than two levels above its foundations. Unlike the organic and spontaneous architectural clusters that covered the landscape at Las Brisas, in Legorreta's proposal, the mountain itself was transformed and abstracted into architecture. Budgetary goals were met by eliminating air conditioning in nearly the entire hotel: as Legorreta explained, "Only sleeping quarters would be mechanically cooled and even in these there would be the option of a simple ceiling fan; the living

The Las Brisas hotel, a scattered organization of bungalows on a hill. Postcard, date unknown.

area of each guest room would be placed outside on a terrace with a hammock and dining place, plants, and a view over the Pacific Ocean—in short, a relaxed living area naturally cooled…"[6] Zooming in on the terraces, some with private pools, we can appreciate the meticulousness of the hotel's formal logic. Rooms are set back into the volume, organizing a smooth progression from dark to light; punctured brise-soleils create different shade conditions. In the middle of each terrace, a non-structural column separates an area for a hammock to hang and the circulation pathway.

Legorreta had employed the building section to solve construction or programmatic requirements in many of his projects, a continuous search for alternatives to the modernist ethos of simply multiplying by stacking. The Celanese Mexicana offices, an early project in which he achieved an unbroken floor slab in a corporate tower, was perhaps one of his most ingenious solutions. By applying an external structural system based on hanging tension members and organizing the plan in four gradually stepped parts (each platform ninety centimeters above the previous segment), he managed to create a work floor that spiraled fluidly upward and that could be freely subdivided by the company. At the Camino Real in Mexico City, we witness an incredibly elegant sequence of staircases, each fourteen to fifteen steps high, that orchestrates gradual move-

Ricardo Legorreta. Balconies at the Hotel Camino Real, Ixtapa.

ment through the public areas of the hotel. In her well-researched PhD thesis, Mara Partida illustrates in detail the beauty of this sequence, in which lobbies, corridors, staircases, and works of art come together in an extremely evocative spatial composition.[7] Legorreta, who always preferred no-nonsense, self-evident rationales, laconically attributed the design of this succession of split levels to "the height difference of about 1,50 meters that exists in between Mariano Escobedo and Leibnitz."[8]

Along with developing interior qualities through sectional compositions, the architect pursued a specific interest in integrating his buildings within the surrounding geography. His earthship-like additions to the Hotel Hacienda in Baja California, from 1972, truly merged architecture and landscape into one single entity. There, at the southern tip of the peninsula, Legorreta felt that "any idea of architecture would be powerless to compete with the natural environment."[9] He decided to bury the required condominium units underground, hidden within an existing sand dune next to the hotel. The cave-like underground spaces, accessible by sunken patios and

The roof as an abstraction of the existing topography, drawing a sharp diagonal line through the forest landscape. Ricardo Legorreta. Casa de Fin de Semana, Valle de Bravo, Mexico, 1973.

lit by skylights, allowed the architect "to leave the landscape untouched."[10] A year later, in 1973, he completed a three-bedroom weekend cottage for his family, set among trees on a hill in Valle de Bravo. The primitive structure is topped by a wood-shingled roof that radically mimics the slope of the existing landscape. This basic formal gesture shapes a cut-out central terrace, establishing the outdoor space as the project's center of gravity. The duplication and abstraction of the existing topography draw a sharp diagonal through the vertical lines of the trees. Despite its small scale, Legorreta published the house in Valle de Bravo both nationally and internationally, illustrating the enthusiasm he felt for the scheme.

The accumulated knowledge of these previous projects comes together in Ixtapa, creating a particular, massive structure that is both architecture and topography at the same time. It reminds us, for example, of Cesar Pelli's project for Sunset Mountain Park in California, Moshe Safdie's Habitat Puerto Rico, and many stepped housing projects developed and built during the late sixties and seventies that used the hillside condition as an alibi to add the diagonal to a modernist idiom defined mainly by horizontal and vertical components. These postwar projects illustrate the paradoxical ambition to be at once megastructural and embedded in a site, combining in a provocative way the abstract geometries of early modernism with ulterior environmental concerns. Legorreta's bold gestures at Ixtapa constitute a powerful example of an architecture that consciously engages with the geographic conditions of the site while avoiding a sentimental contextual approach.

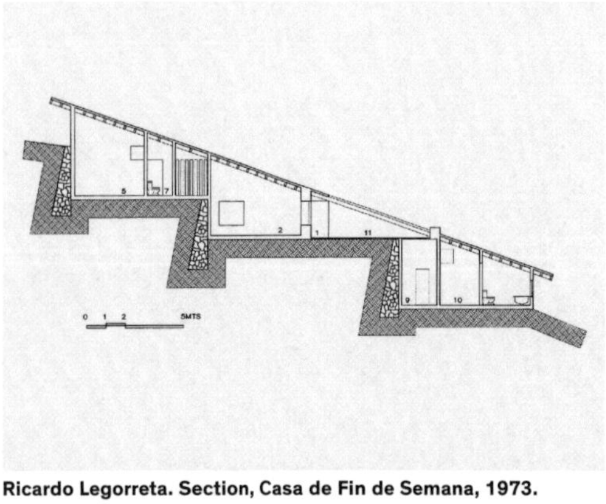

Ricardo Legorreta. Section, Casa de Fin de Semana, 1973.

Cave-like condominium units on the beach side of the Hotel Hacienda. Ricardo Legorreta. Hotel Hacienda, Cabo San Lucas, Mexico, 1973.

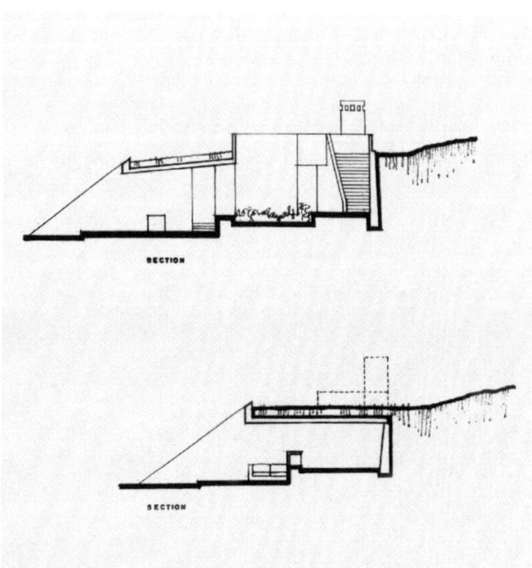

Ricardo Legorreta. Section, Hotel Hacienda, 1973.

1 Wayne Attoe in Wayne Attoe, ed., *The Architecture of Ricardo Legorreta* (Austin, TX: University of Texas Press, 1990), 154.
2 Victor R. Zevallos, "Camino Real," *Architectural Forum* 129, no. 4 (November 1968): 89.
3 Quoted in Miquel Adria and José Castillo, eds., *Ricardo Legorreta: El verdadero lujo está en el espacio* (Mexico City: Arquine, 2013), 28. Author's translation.
4 Quoted in Attoe, 151.
5 Quoted in Attoe, 151.
6 Quoted in Attoe, 154.
7 Mara Partida, "Hotel Camino Real. Cruce de Artistas y Arquitectos en la Ciudad de Mexico, 1968" (PhD thesis, Escola Tècnica Superior d'Arquitectura de Barcelona, 2004).
8 Quoted in Adria and Castillo, *Ricardo Legorreta*, 26. Author's translation.
9 Quoted in C. Ray Smith, "Low Density in the Dunes," *Progressive Architecture* 57, no. 9 (September 1976): 68.
10 Smith, 68.

TOPOGRAPHIC ARCHITECTURE KENNETH FRAMPTON'S INTEREST IN THE GROUND

Véronique Patteeuw

"It is said that architects always design the same building. In a sense I have always rewritten the same essay."[1]

In 1980, just a few months before the opening of the first International Architecture Exhibition of the Venice Biennale, British architectural historian Kenneth Frampton resigned from the curatorial team. His co-curators, Paolo Portoghesi, Robert A. M. Stern, Charles Jencks, Christian Norberg-Schulz, and Vincent Scully, had settled on an approach that emphasized the glorification of the past and positioned postmodernism as an architectural style of historicist eclecticism, in fierce opposition to Frampton's ideology.[2] Although Frampton was critical of the legacy of the modern movement, he shared Jurgen Habermas's commitment to "the unfinished project of modernity"[3] and argued for an architecture that would resist the universalizing hegemony of the postmodern times he was witnessing.

Frampton's "criticism from within," as Léa-Catherine Szacka has suggested, prepared the field for alternative sensibilities in architecture through which his interest in the ground

Aris Konstantinidis anchors his weekend house in Anavissos, Greece, to its ground, a bare shore in an isolated setting. 1962.

becomes apparent.[4] In reaction to impending universalization, the historian argued for the specificities of place. In reaction to the postmodern reduction of architecture to images, he reclaimed expressive forms of architectural structure and tectonics. In reaction to the modernist *tabula rasa*, he emphasized the importance of site and topography. Frampton elaborated his vision in a sequence of texts, articles, books, lectures, and teaching modules,[5] an exploration that had started a decade before his involvement in Venice and would climax in his seminal essay "Towards a Critical Regionalism: Six Points for an Architecture of Resistance," published in 1983.[6]

In Frampton's call for the tactile instead of the visual, the tectonic rather than the scenographic, and the hybrid over the homogeneous, one finds evidence that ground and topography were leading notions for the historian. In the first point of both his original text and the extended versions that followed, he argued for an embedded architecture, proposing a radical alternative to absolute placelessness, and in doing so, elevated the specifics of the ground to an essential aspect of the art of building. He argued that a certain form of resistance seemed to develop in a climate where culture became a global concept. As such, Frampton aimed to rescue architecture from the many manipulations of history by providing it with a solid rootedness. But how did Frampton apprehend this rootedness? Was it essential to the architecture he promoted, a mere provocation against the so-called "presence of the past," or a mechanism in his attempt to reposition architecture ideologically?

Earth Work Versus Roof Work

We may find a first set of answers by taking a closer look at the concept of "critical regionalism" itself. As is well known, Frampton did not invent the

The title page of Kenneth Frampton's essay "Prospects for a Critical Regionalism" in *Perspecta* 20 (1983).

Robust columns mark the architectural perimeter of a rational plan. Aris Konstantinidis. Weekend house, Anavissos, 1962.

term, but borrowed it from Alexander Tzonis and Liane Lefaivre, who coined it in their 1981 article "The Grid and the Pathway," about the work of the Greek architects Suzana Antonakakis and Dimitris Antonakakis.[7] Frampton's interest in Greek architecture dates from his first visit to the Acropolis, in 1959, when he discovered the work of Dimitris Pikionis. Then a relatively unknown architect, Pikionis received the commission to design a new pathway, rest stops, and viewing platforms on the Acropolis site in the early 1950s.[8] Pikionis realized his meandering pathway in fragments of marble and stone pavement in different shapes and sizes, carefully positioning steps, benches, and viewing platforms so each element dissolves in the overall setting. The intervention appears to be an ancient, accidental trail integrated into the conditions of the surrounding landscape. Manufactured by craftsmen who were able to adapt Pikionis's design to the specifics of the site, the pathway proposed a delicate ambulatory experience.[9] (Hélène Binet captures this quality in a series of photographs produced in the late 1980s.) For Frampton it referred directly to a certain sensibility of the ground: "You can not only see [the ground]; you can read it with your feet."[10]

If Pikionis's pathway exemplifies Frampton's fascination with what we might call "earth work," the oeuvre of another Greek architect represents a valuable counterpart.[11] Aris Konstantinidis, born half a century after Pikionis, proposes a less sensitive but more rational way of intervening on the ground. His weekend house in Anavissos, not far from Athens, is an extraordinary example. Placed on a bare shore in an isolated setting, it anchors itself to the ground with robust, massive columns while enabling the earth to run freely

Carefully positioned fragments of marble and stone create a meandering pathway. Hélène Binet, photographer. Dimitris Pikionis, architect. Landscaping around the Acropolis (1950s), Athens, 1989.

underneath an elegant roof, which marks the architectural perimeter of the rational plan. The stereotomy of the stonework underlines the building's relation to the landscape.[12]

Representing seemingly opposite architectural approaches, Pikionis's pathway and Konstantinidis's house defined a dialectical set of interests for the young Frampton. While the pathway proposed a natural melding of landscape and architecture that laid the project within the site, the weekend house suggested a method of forming space that subsumed the site in the rationality of the plan. These two Greek examples demonstrated the tension between an architecture exploiting the irregularities and ambiguities of a landscape on the one hand and a form of structured reasoning of that landscape on the other hand, a tension between "earth work" and "roof work." It was precisely this tension that inspired Frampton in his quest for an architecture of resistance.[13]

Laid-In Architecture

If "Towards a Critical Regionalism" reads as an attempt to counter universalization with architecture, what specific architecture did Frampton have in mind? He specifically pleads for an architecture that "involves a more directly dialectical relation with nature than the more abstract, formal traditions of modern avant-garde architecture allow."[14] After several more philosophical explorations, he spatializes his ideas in the last two points of the text, arguing for the importance of the topographic and climatological conditions of a site, the tectonics of architectural construction, and the tactile

Pikionis's intervention appears to be an ancient, accidental trail through the surrounding landscape. Hélène Binet, photographer. Dimitris Pikionis, architect. Landscaping around the Acropolis (1950s), 1989.

sensibility of architecture. The ground, as in "topography," "site," and "inscription," is the first item addressed in point 5. For Frampton, the ground can be both a window onto a natural condition and a frame for the historical layers of a specific place. Before addressing Mario Botta and his notion of "building the site," the historian makes an appeal for *bounded architecture*, architecture that has little affinity to the freestanding architectural object, but which is inscribed in the topographic, geological, or agricultural history of the site—in other words, a sort of laid-in architecture clearly opposed, as he claims in the text, to a modern approach. "The bulldozing of an irregular topography into a flat site is clearly a technocratic gesture which aspires to a condition of absolute *placelessness*," he writes, "whereas the terracing of the same site to receive the stepped form of a building is an engagement in the act of 'cultivating' the site."[15]

But are all laid-in buildings, according to Frampton, situated on terraced sites and realized in stepped forms? Before and after the publication of "Towards a Critical Regionalism" in *The Anti-Aesthetic*, Frampton wrote several other versions of his text, which together show the development of his theoretical framework. For example, while the version published in *The Anti-Aesthetic* omits many examples, "Prospects for a Critical Regionalism," a text published in *Perspecta*, also in 1983, cites numerous projects and

Álvaro Siza's swimming pool complex in Leça de Palmeira, Portugal, questions the boundaries between landscape and architecture. 1966.

architects exemplifying his interest in the ground. An example that recurs across these texts is the Portuguese architect Álvaro Siza and his swimming pool complex in Leça de Palmeira.

Set along the northern coastline of Matosinhos, a small town to the north of Porto, the Leça de Palmeira complex is hardly visible from the road. Conceived of as a pathway slowly descending from the coastal road and passing through changing rooms, set parallel to an existing, long seawall, the complex offers a sensory experience even within the building. With no views, the ocean becomes audible. Continuing toward the pools, the pathway dematerializes; Siza's interventions in the irregular landscape of the rocks are limited to platforms, stairs, walls, and dead ends. While the inclined ramps and walls protect from wind, the materials—reinforced concrete, stone paving, treated Riga wood, and copper roofing—allow the complex to disappear into the landscape. Inspired by the work of Finnish architect Alvar Aalto, Siza was able to ground his building in the configuration of the topography: it is both delicately layered and laid into the site. For Frampton, Siza's "pieces" are exemplary in proposing an "extraordinary sensitivity towards local materials, craft work, and, above all, to the subtleties of local light."[16]

Siza's architecture is just one of many examples cited by the historian. In the *Perspecta* text, he also references the Scandinavian architecture of Jørn Utzon and Aalto before introducing the work of J. A. Coderch in Spain, Dolf Schnebli and Botta in Switzerland, and Gino Valle, Carlo Scarpa, and Luigi Snozzi (with Botta) in Italy. For Frampton, their architectural approaches testify in each specific case to the regional and local conditions of the site

While inclined ramps and walls protect from wind, the materials—reinforced concrete, stone paving, treated Riga wood, and copper roofing—allow the complex to disappear into the landscape. Álvaro Siza. Swimming pool complex, Leça de Palmeira, 1966.

and use specificity at the core of their designs, as he would write in more general terms in "Towards a Critical Regionalism": "This inscription, which arises out of 'in-laying' the building into the site, has many levels of significance, for it has a capacity to embody, in built form, the prehistory of the place, its archeological past and its subsequent cultivation and transformation across time. Through this layering into the site the idiosyncrasies of place find their expression without falling into sentimentality."[17]

Peripheral Grounds

But Frampton's search for a grounded architecture also needs to be understood in a different light. Within the context of the powerful winds of a decontextualized postmodernity, Frampton aimed to give attention to architects who had been relegated to the periphery of a system centered around star figures working in specific areas in Europe. For the historian, then, the periphery was also geographic: the topographical conditions of peripheral European regions (Greece, Spain, and Portugal, but also the Swiss Ticino region) enabled him to explore practices with alternative stances toward postmodernism. His interest went beyond the borders of the old continent. As a technical editor for *Architectural Design* (between 1962 and 1965), he ambitioned an "encyclopedic" editorial policy that resulted in thirty-one issues of *AD* focusing on the development of modern architecture in peripheral situations, including extensive features on non-European territories like Chile, Brazil, and Mexico. Although the magazine still covered the United States comprehensively, its predominant geographical focus shifted under Frampton's direction to continental Europe and Latin America,

which were featured in extended articles on specific regions, architects, and single buildings.

Frampton's attention to these peripheral conditions allowed him to explore local environments, vernacular elements, and material cultures. In "Prospects for a Critical Regionalism" and in subsequent reworked versions of his *Modern Architecture: A Critical History*, the British historian cites projects by the Argentinean architect Amancio Williams, the Brazilian architect Clorindo Testa, and the Venezuelan architect Carlos Raúl Villanueva, as well as the "sensual and earthbound architecture" of Mexico's Luis Barragán, whose unification of architecture, landscape, and gardening is the basis of the topographic dimension of critical regionalism: for Frampton, while Barragán remained committed to "large, almost inscrutable abstract planes set in the landscape," his houses "are nothing if not topographic."[18] Frampton continued advancing his interest in peripheral conditions in several edited publications and essays.[19] The list of his writings is long, his conviction strong: "It is my contention that Critical Regionalism continues to flourish sporadically within the cultural fissures that articulate in unexpected ways the continents of Europe and America. These borderline manifestations may be characterized, after Abraham Moles, as the 'interstices of freedom.'"[20]

Just as his *Modern Architecture* argued that architectural modernism was as much a struggle for social and political expression as an aesthetic statement, in these works, Frampton constantly looks beneath the aesthetic surface of buildings in search of deeper meanings. His interest in the ground—its tactility and sensuality—enabled a significant number of practices to come out of the shadows

Álvaro Siza. Swimming pool complex, Leça de Palmeira, 1966.

both in Europe and in Latin America. We might even wonder if critical regionalism was not also about architectural sensibilities that have traveled through cultures, from one territory to the next,[21] from one ground to another.

Uncovering the Earth

Topographic architecture might generally be comprehended in different ways: as a compositional understanding of the ground figure of the project, as an interest in the cultural and material histories of a specific site, or as an awareness of the technical constraints and opportunities that a site can imply. For Frampton, however, there is still another aspect crucial to the term: topographic architecture needs to be situated within an ideological perspective. Frampton was clearly not interested in sentimental architecture. His Marxist reaction to universal capitalization, and his refusal of Western architecture's hegemonic turn toward history,[22] let him develop a theoretical apparatus that would enable an architecture of resistance. As such, critical regionalism proposed a set of disciplinary categories that aimed at understanding architecture beyond (aesthetic) universalization, as a set of political values.

But if Frampton had originally set out these categories to enact a political agenda, the text's critical fortune has blurred this objective. Critical regionalism became all too soon a historical document, understood as a poetic, a-critical, and apolitical interest in peripheral conditions. In an epoch when architecture needs a renewed frame of values, Frampton's engaged theory of the discipline is more than ever food for thought.

This text was written in parallel to the preparation of "Critical Regionalism Revisited," *OASE* 103, ed. Tom Avermaete, Véronique Patteeuw, Léa-Catherine Szacka, and Hans Teerds (2019).

1 Kenneth Frampton, "Critical Regionalism Revisited" (lecture, University of Washington, Seattle, May 15, 2013).

2 It is no coincidence that Frampton published his seminal book *Modern Architecture: A Critical History*, a plea for a critical examination of modern architecture, the same year he resigned from the Biennale. See Kenneth Frampton, *Modern Architecture: A Critical History* (London: Thames & Hudson, 1980).

3 Frampton to Portoghesi, letter of resignation, April 25, 1980, Biennale di Venezia, Archivio Storico delle Arti Contemporanee, fondo storico, b. 658. For a more thorough analysis of Frampton's position, see Léa-Catherine Szacka, "Criticism from Within: Kenneth Frampton and the Retreat from Postmodernism," *OASE* 98 (2016): 110–16; and Stylianos Giamarelos, "Intersecting Itineraries beyond the Strada Novissima: The Converging Authorship of Critical Regionalism," *Architectural Histories* 4, no. 1 (2016): 1–18.

4 See Szacka, "Criticism from Within."

5 One could argue this sequence started as early as December 1971 with the publication of "America 1960–1970" in "The City as an Artifact," *Casabella* 359/360. See Marine Urbain, "Eclosion d'une pensée. Le régionalisme critique de Kenneth Frampton, 1983" (master's thesis, Université libre de Bruxelles, 2017).

6 Kenneth Frampton, "Towards a Critical Regionalism: Six Points for an Architecture of Resistance," in *The Anti-Aesthetic: Essays on Postmodern Culture*, ed. Hal Foster (Port Townsend, WA: Bay Press, 1983).

7 Kenneth Frampton, "Towards an Agonistic Architecture" (lecture, SCI-Arc, Los Angeles, December 4, 2013).

8 See Kenneth Frampton, Agni Pikioni, and Hannele Grönland, eds., *Dimitris Pikionis 1887–1968: A Greek Architect* (Helsinki: Museum of Finnish Architecture, 1993).

9 See Nicholas Kehagias, "Paving a Greek Path to a Western Monument," personal website, accessed January 8, 2019, http://www.nicholaskehagias.com/the-acropolis-pavement/; and Dimitris Pikionis, *Dimitris Pikionis, Architect 1887–1968: A Sentimental Topography* (London: Architectural Association, 1989).

10 Frampton, "Towards an Agonistic Architecture."

11 Frampton discusses the work of Konstantinidis in Kenneth Frampton, "The Isms of Contemporary Architecture," *Architectural Design* 52 (1982): 60–83.

12 Konstantinidis elaborates on such connections in his 1975 book *Elements of Self-Knowledge: Towards a True Architecture*, using his own photographs to supply a series of examples.

13 For further discussion of this dialectical tension, see Frampton, "Critical Regionalism Revisited."

14 Frampton, "Towards a Critical Regionalism," 26.

15 Frampton, "Towards a Critical Regionalism," 26.

16 Kenneth Frampton, "Prospects for a Critical Regionalism," *Perspecta* 20 (1983): 151.

17 Frampton, "Towards a Critical Regionalism," 26.

18 Frampton, "Prospects for a Critical Regionalism," 152–53.

19 For more on Frampton's interest in the periphery, see "Place, Production and Reality," *Architecture in Greece* (1977); "Mario Botta and the School of the Ticino," *Oppositions* 14 (1978); *A New Wave of Japanese Architecture*, exhibition catalogue (New York: Institute for Architecture and Urban Studies, 1978); "Works or Panos Koulermos," *Architecture and Urbanism* (May 1979); "Notes on the Architecture of Panos Koulermos," *Architecture in Greece* 17 (1983); Kenneth Frampton, ed., *Tadao Ando: Buildings Projects Writings* (New York: Rizzoli, 1984); "Tre opere di Panos Koulermos: Una mostra allo studio Marconi a Milano," *Casabella* (July–August 1984); "Entre el racionalismo y el regionalismo: la obra de Martorell, Bohigas y Mackay, 1954-1984," in *Martorell, Bohigas, Mackay* (Barcelona: Xarait Ediciones / Electa, 1985); Kenneth Frampton, ed., *The Architecture of Hiromi Fujii*, exhibition catalogue (New York: Rizzoli, 1987); Kenneth Frampton, ed., *Kengo Kuma: Complete Works* (New York: Thames & Hudson, 2013); "The Work of Rogelio Salmona," *A + U: Architecture and Urbanism* (March 2008): 28–33; Kenneth Frampton, "Plan Form and Topography in the Work of Kashef Chowdhury," in *Kashef Chowdhury: The Friendship Centre, Gaibandha, Bangladesh* (Zurich: Park Books, 2016); and Kenneth Frampton, "The Architect as Amateur: The Studio of Wang Shu and Lu Wengyu," in *Wang Shu Amateur Architecture Studio* (Zurich: Lars Müller, 2017).

20 Frampton, "Prospects for a Critical Regionalism," 149.

21 See Giamarelos, "Intersecting Itineraries," 2.

22 It is important to note that one critique of this aspect of critical regionalism is readily apparent: while Frampton made a case for an architecture of resistance to an imposed power from above, and situated architectural approaches outside the center, his Western concept was imposed upon the architecture he highlighted, often limiting the varied architectural production of the above-mentioned countries to singular practices.

"The first space for living was the cave. The first house was the hollow mound of earth.
To build meant: to gather and layer building material [and] mass, around voids for air [and] living [and] space. …
The technique of architect and sculptor was similar. …
The architectural design concerns itself with 'space' as its raw material and with articulated room as its product. …
The architect has finally discovered the medium of his art: SPACE."[1]

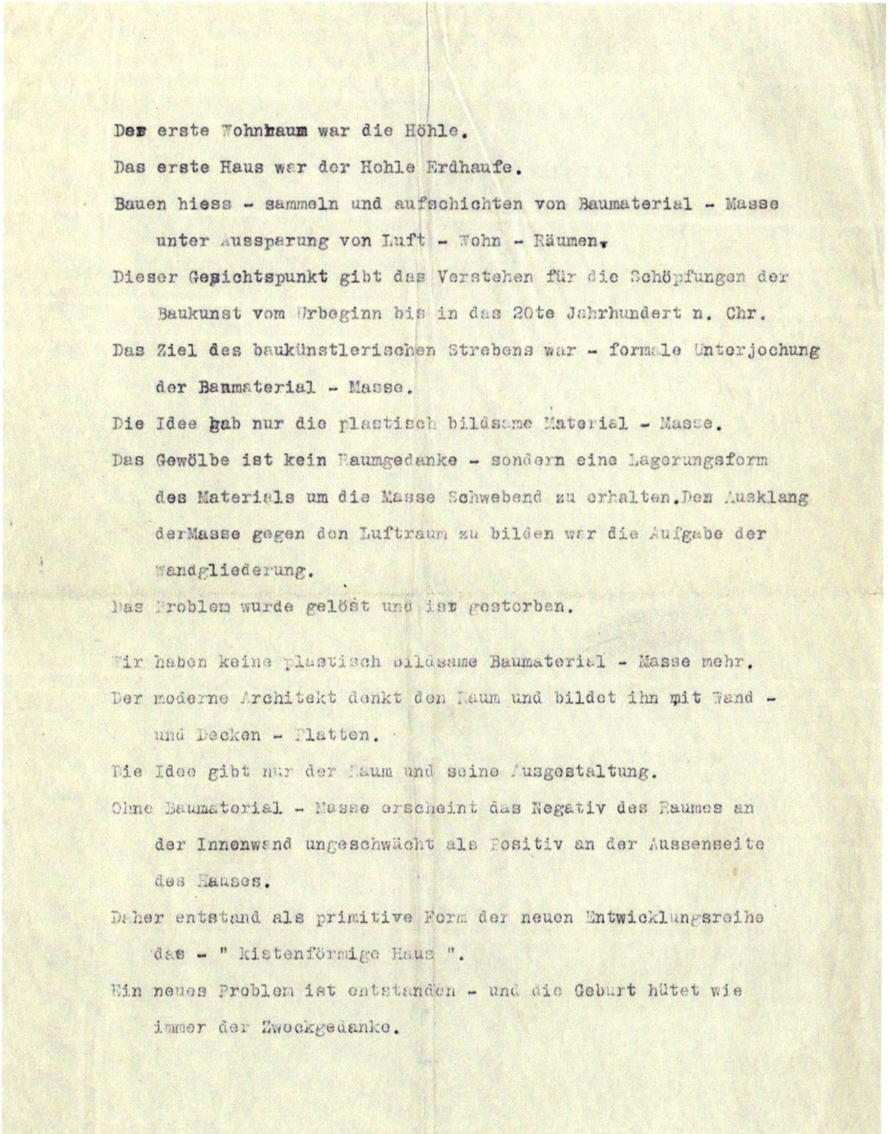

Der erste Wohnraum war die Höhle.

Das erste Haus war der Hohle Erdhaufe.

Bauen hiess - sammeln und aufschichten von Baumaterial - Masse unter Aussparung von Luft - Wohn - Räumen.

Dieser Gesichtspunkt gibt das Verstehen für die Schöpfungen der Baukunst vom Urbeginn bis in das 20te Jahrhundert n. Chr.

Das Ziel des baukünstlerischen Strebens war - formale Unterjochung der Baumaterial - Masse.

Die Idee gab nur die plastisch bildsame Material - Masse.

Das Gewölbe ist kein Raumgedanke - sondern eine Lagerungsform des Materials um die Masse Schwebend zu erhalten.Den Ausklang derMasse gegen den Luftraum zu bilden war die Aufgabe der Wandgliederung.

Das Problem wurde gelöst und ist gestorben.

Wir haben keine plastisch bildsame Baumaterial - Masse mehr.

Der moderne Architekt denkt den Raum und bildet ihn mit Wand - und Decken - Platten.

Die Idee gibt nur der Raum und seine Ausgestaltung.

Ohne Baumaterial - Masse erscheint das Negativ des Raumes an der Innenwand ungeschwächt als Positiv an der Aussenseite des Hauses.

Daher entstand als primitive Form der neuen Entwicklungsreihe das - " kistenförmige Haus ".

Ein neues Problem ist entstanden - und die Geburt hütet wie immer der Zweckgedanke.

The original, German version of R. M. Schindler's "Moderne Architektur: ein Programm," 1912.

Written in Vienna in 1912, a place and time marked by some of the most radical cultural shifts of the last century, Rudolf M. Schindler's "Moderne Architektur: ein Programm" describes the origins of architecture and offers two directives for the architecture of that moment: first, that architecture must concern itself not with the object, but with space; and second, that architecture is to be from and of the earth.

Ten years later, Schindler built his own, seminal house in Los Angeles. He had moved to America to work with Frank Lloyd Wright, and had overseen Wright's studio during the master's long voyages to Japan. He was in Los Angeles supervising the construction of Wright's first and most significant commission there, the Hollyhock House, built for the oil heiress Aline Barnsdall. He had also traveled throughout the American Southwest, reporting to Richard Neutra back in Vienna that "the only buildings that testify to any true feeling of the earth from which they spring are the ancient adobe buildings" there.[2] The house he would design for himself, constructed between February and June 1922, is a building as radical today as it was almost a century ago. "The basic idea

Above and right: The entry and living space of Geoffrey Bawa's Polontalawa Estate Bungalow. The main roof structure is supported by boulders. Near Nikarawetiya, Sri Lanka, 1963–65.

was to give each person his own room—instead of the usual distribution," he explained in a letter to his parents-in-law in 1921.[3] He elaborated on this atypical arrangement in an article in the journal *T-Square*, published in 1932, in which he describes the house as "a cooperative dwelling for two young couples ... [where] rooms for specialized purposes [have] been abandoned." "Instead," he continues, "each person receives a large private studio; each couple a common entrance hall and bath. Open porches on the roof are used for sleeping. An enclosed patio for each couple, with an out-of-door fireplace, serves the purposes of an ordinary living room.... One kitchen is planned for both couples."[4] Architecturally, Schindler combines in his house the idea of the "cave" (the concrete floors and walls on three sides of the spaces) with the idea of the "tent" (the delicate wood, glass, and canvas enclosures of the fourth walls), anticipating two distinct positions in the architecture of the coming century.

The connection between nature and architecture was central to modernism. Two distinct strategies exist: buildings that, like those of Neutra or Ludwig Mies van der Rohe, extend architectural elements out into their surrounding landscapes, ultimately controlling their sites, and buildings that draw the surrounding landscape into the architectural space.

In many cases, the dialogue in the latter approach is abstract: Schindler, for example, would at times stain the plywood of his built-in furniture in tones that matched the surrounding greenery. More surprising examples can be found in the house that Charles and Ray Eames built for themselves, Case Study House 8. The house, as much a "tent" as was technically possible at the time (the Eameses speak of a "kite," a delicate structure with the thinnest possible enclosure[5]), is precisely set between the toe of a slope and a row of eucalyptus trees, planted when the species was introduced from Australia to Southern California as a possible source for railroad timber. Two unexpectedly romantic

The entry to the cave-like Elrod House (1968), seen from the street. John Lautner, architect. Leland Y. Lee, photographer. Palm Springs, California, 1977.

moments connect the house to its site. A solid panel facing the living room terrace that at first appears to be cement board with vertical streaks is, in fact, an atmospheric photograph of the site depicting the surrounding trees. Inside the house, the large two-story wood wall in the living room is Australian tallowwood (*Eucalyptus microcorys*)—a machined echo of the row of trees in front of the house.

Other examples are more direct. In his early Textile Block houses, in Los Angeles, Frank Lloyd Wright mixed soil from the project sites into his concrete, an effort to unite earth and building with technically disastrous results (this severely weakened the concrete). At Fallingwater, the rock—from which the house grows and to which it is anchored—is the actual hearth of the fireplace, the literal and physical center of the house. The rock rises slightly above the stone floor to connect the fire to the famed waterfall. At Oscar Niemeyer's Casa das Canoas, the rock is a more central element, organizing not only the house's plan and section but also the thin, white, amorphous roof, the curved solid and diaphanous glazed walls, the greenery, and the views. The second house

The rugged terrain that inserts itself into the Elrod House. John Lautner, architect. Leland Y. Lee, photographer. Circa 1970.

Albert Frey designed for himself is the smallest imaginable pavilion set amid the rocks above Palm Springs, California. It is also organized around a massive boulder, separating areas on different levels for sleeping, dining and working, and living. The lightness of the structure—a most delicate steel and glass enclosure carrying a thin roof of corrugated steel—belies the harshness of the desert climate in summer and winter. Built around the same time as Frey's house, Geoffrey Bawa's Polontalawa Estate Bungalow is one of the great Sri Lankan architect's most unusual projects.[6] Bawa's buildings generally show an affinity with their sites that reflects his interest in landscape architecture—his career began with him reshaping his own large country estate, Lunuganga, before he decided to study architecture at the Architectural Association—as well as his respect for the land, rocks, and trees that are part of the culture he was born into. At Polontalawa, public areas including the kitchen and living spaces are set between a simple plinth, which grows from the ground, and an expansive, protective roof supported by massive, sculptural concrete beams, which in turn rest on a series of extraordinary boulders, around whichflows the space. The rocks are of the site and of the house.

It is unclear if John Lautner knew Bawa's Polontalawa project.[7] Lautner was famously an apprentice and respected collaborator of Wright's from 1933 to 1938, in the years that Wright worked on Fallingwater and while he extracted his Taliesin West from the Sonoran desert. Lautner also knew and respected Schindler and

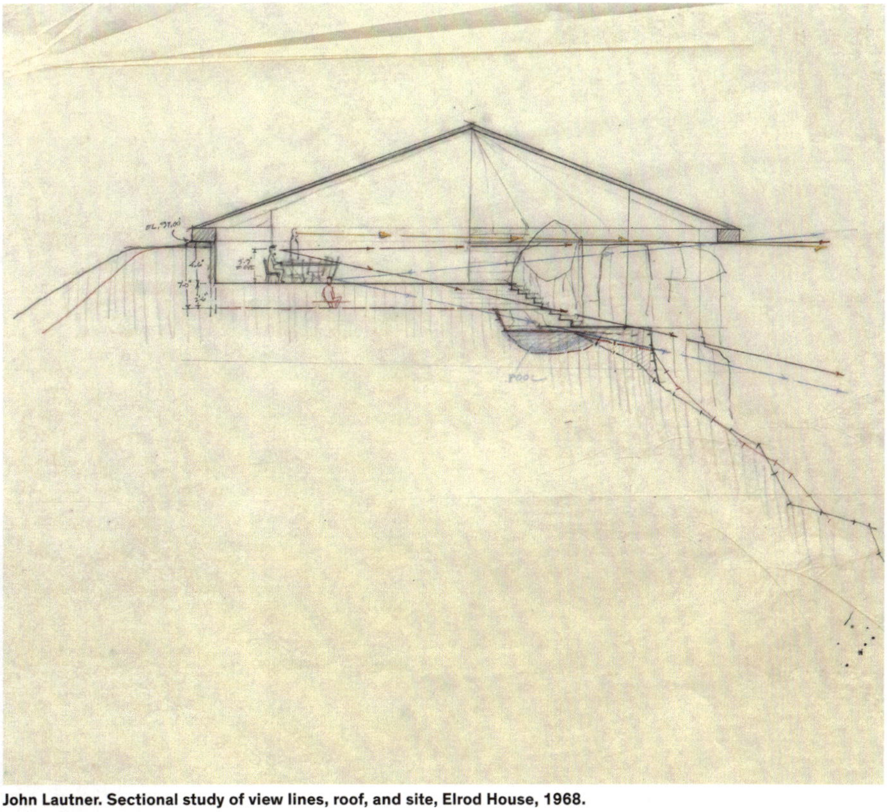

John Lautner. Sectional study of view lines, roof, and site, Elrod House, 1968.

his writings and would have been familiar with Schindler's article "Space Architecture," published in February 1934 in the *Dune Forum* (edited at the time by Schindler's estranged wife, Pauline Schindler). In this article, Schindler articulates many of the thoughts first expressed in his 1912 text. Lautner also knew Frey and visited Niemeyer in Brazil, though not until the late 1980s, after Niemeyer returned from his European exile in 1985.

Lautner's formal language, and in particular his later, fluid work, is shaped equally by twentieth-century developments in structural engineering (including the work of Eduardo Torroja; Félix Candela, with whom Lautner collaborated on the Hope Residence; and Frei Otto, with whom he corresponded) and his almost obsessive photography of forms of nature—landscapes, rock formations, clouds, lakes. Lautner used his camera in the way that other architects use a sketchbook, and his archives house thousands of these nature studies. The seismographic reading of his sites, registering their every subtlety, would shape each of his projects. Lautner's efforts to incorporate elements from the surrounding nature into his architecture are visible in projects as distinct as the Pearlman Mountain Cabin, where he used tree trunks as the building's structure, echoing the surrounding forest, and the celebrated Arango House, in Acapulco, Mexico, where the continuous edge of water surrounding the main, open living space visually merges with the water of the Pacific Ocean below.

Lautner's Elrod House is built in the mountains above Palm Springs. Early in the project, Lautner noticed the tops of boulders emerging from the site and proposed to excavate the

Above and right: Boulders feature as interior commodities in the Elrod House. John Lautner, architect. Leland Y. Lee, photographer. 1977 and ca. 1970.

ground about eight feet (2.4 meters) to fully expose and integrate these into his building. Thus, the site's geology is almost violently thrust through the floor and into the circular space. A concrete wall encircles the perimeter; the roof is a shallow concrete cone, with a massive concrete tension ring that supports nine wide concrete blades radiating from the center. Between these blades, various skylights open to the mountains, the horizon, and the sky. The house certainly is one of the most interesting "caves" of the twentieth century, to return to Schindler's terminology. Frey, however, was convinced that his own house, a "tent" sitting lightly on the ground a few miles away, was the right approach to such a site, and that Lautner's was not. "It doesn't make sense to have heavy concrete overhead," Frey complained. "Why lift all that heavy stuff up there? . . . I always liked the lightness of things.

The main living space of the Elrod House in its original condition. Leland Y. Lee, photographer. 1968.

The sheet-metal people put up the roof (of my house); it took them a day. And then I put these panels up on the insulation myself. If you have concrete, they actually have to build a whole structure to support it. It doesn't make sense. Concrete is fine in relation to the ground. It's an earth material."[8]

A few years later, in the early 1970s, Lautner worked on various unbuilt schemes for a small vacation house for himself in Three Rivers, California, in the foothills of the Sierra Nevada. The site was on the banks of the Kaweah River and strewn with massive boulders. Though the house has a different relation to its rocky site—in one scheme, the small house is lofted on massive concrete pillars above the rocks; in another, the house is precariously perched on top of a tall boulder—the boulders are the foundation and starting point for his design. Here, Lautner may be the furthest away from Schindler's 1912 dictum, well outside the "tent" and "cave" polemic. But his project, nevertheless, begins and ends with his site, the ground, the earth.

Above and right: At the Frey House, a boulder seems to interrupt, rather than support, the building's tent-like steel frame. Albert Frey, architect. Julius Shulman, photographer. Palm Springs, California, 1964.

1 The original manifesto is held in the R. M. Schindler papers, Architecture & Design Collection, Art, Design & Architecture Museum, University of California, Santa Barbara. Author's translation. Schindler's 1912 text underwent many changes. Schindler himself made notes on the text for a series of lectures he gave in Chicago in 1916 and Los Angeles in 1921, and he translated it to English around 1932, making it more technical, more prosaic, and less poetic than the original (the mound, for example, is no longer of "earth"—*Erde*—but of "adobe"). Over the years, this 1932 English version became known as the Schindler manifesto. According to Judith Sheine, "Schindler's 1932 translation was made in light of his later experiences. His attack on 'functionalism' and focus on 'space' were emphasized in his 1934 article 'Space Architecture,' in which he contrasts his work with that of the International Stylist branch of modernism." Judith Sheine, letter to the author, 2014.

2 "Die einzigen Bauten, die von wirklichem Gefühl für den Boden der sie trägt zeugen, sind die alten Lehmziegelbauten (der ersten Einwanderer)." R. M. Schindler, letter to Richard Neutra, December 1920 or January 1921. Translated in August Sarnitz, *R. M. Schindler, Architekt, 1887–1953* (Vienna: Christian Brandstätter Verlag & Edition, 1986), 204.

3 R. M. Schindler, letter to Mr. and Mrs. Edmund J. Gibling, November 26, 1921, quoted in Kathryn Smith, *Schindler House* (Santa Monica, CA: Hennessey + Ingalls, 2010), 19.

4 R. M. Schindler, "A Cooperative Dwelling," *T-Square* 2 (February 1932), quoted in Robert Sweeney and Judith Sheine, *Schindler, Kings Road, and Southern California Modernism* (Berkeley: University of California Press, 2012), 15.

5 For example, a 1950 *Architectural Forum* article describing the house is titled "Life in a Chinese Kite."

6 The Polontalawa bungalow was done in collaboration with the Danish architect Ulrik Plesner, a longtime associate.

7 The Polontalawa bungalow was published for the first time in February 1966 in the *Architectural Review* ("Ceylon - Seven New Buildings"), and again in 1965 in the Danish magazine *Arkitekten* ("Arbejder pa Ceylon"). Further, in 1967, the Hawaii Chapter of the American Institute of Architects awarded Bawa the Pan Pacific Citation; at the time, Lautner was working on various, mostly unbuilt projects for the Hilo Campus of the University of Hawaii.

8 Albert Frey, interview by Jennifer Golub, in Jennifer Golub, *Albert Frey / Houses 1+2* (New York: Princeton Architectural Press, 1998), 78–79.

The doctoral thesis of Luis Moreno Mansilla, written while he was a fellow at the Spanish Academy in Rome, retraces the travels of a series of famous architects during their grand tours of Italy. Walking through Villa Adriana, for example, the young Mansilla would compare the drawings made by Eugène Viollet-le-Duc, Le Corbusier, or Álvaro Siza, and would make an effort to see the place through their eyes, to understand their different concerns and the way they experienced and conceptualized these sites and, by extension, the world.[1]

Despite elaborating on the obsessions of a diverse group of architects, Mansilla's thesis, like most dissertations, is indeed a compendium of his own preoccupations; like any of us, when writing about others, Mansilla is ultimately writing about himself. In that regard, it is telling that the thread that resurfaces most consistently, perhaps because many of the sites revisited are ruins, is the blurred boundary between the natural and the artificial. Mansilla's interest in this threshold is

The process of ruination softens the forms of the Baths of Caracalla to a point where they become akin to nature. Eugène Viollet-le-Duc. View of the Baths of Caracalla, Ruins of the Frigidarium, Rome, 1836–37.

evident in his discussion of a series of drawings by Viollet-le-Duc, namely his rendition of the Baths of Caracalla and his studies of the crater of Mount Etna. Seen through Viollet-le-Duc's eyes, the softened massiveness of the baths as they devolve into nature is akin to the roughly faceted geometry of the volcano. Later, Mansilla writes, "When the ruins pretend to be nature and the mountains disguise themselves as architecture, one finds himself in an unexplored territory, as if inside the glass that sometimes keeps them apart."[2] Quite revealingly, according to Mansilla, Viollet-le-Duc's persistently stated intention to "carve his own path in stone" resulted not just from his maverick persona, but ultimately from his belief that architecture was already there to be found in nature. Mansilla's reading of Viollet-le-Duc then insinuates, I'd like to propose, that the work of the architect can be likened to

In Viollet-le-Duc's many drawings of the crater of Mount Etna, the mountain becomes geometric, almost an architecture. *Cratère de l'Etna*, June 1836.

that of someone like Michelangelo, who labored the blocks of marble for his unfinished *Slaves* in an attempt to uncover their potential.

A positioning of sculpture as a possible model for mediation between the natural and the artificial is indeed hinted at in other passages of the book, such as the one that describes Le Corbusier's collaboration with the Marseillais mathematician Edward Trouin. Obsessed with the legend of Mary Magdalene, who supposedly ended her life as a hermit in the Sainte-Baume mountain range, Trouin had purchased a million square meters of land near Plan d'Aups intending to build a subterranean basilica in honor of the saint. Trouin's idea, which Le Corbusier turned into geometry, consisted of boring through the mountain, carving its insides from north to south with a series of connected chambers that would culminate in openings toward the Mediterranean Sea and its light.

While Le Corbusier and Trouin's unrealized fantasy to carve a mountain may seem to be a footnote or historical anomaly within the field of architecture, the project in fact relates closely to a certain lineage of sculpture. To name just two instances in such a lineage, Eduardo Chillida pursued for several decades a project to produce a cubic void inside the sacred mountain

Eduardo Chillida had a lifelong obsession to hollow out a mountain in order to create a sacred space. *Mount Tindaya*, 1985–.

of Tindaya in Tenerife, a plan that the inhabitants of the island are still entertaining, and James Turrell has devoted the latter half of his career and his life to the hollowing out of the Roden Crater, in northern Arizona.

For Mansilla, a sculptural attitude such as the one found at the Sainte-Baume church is relevant because it allows architecture to imagine itself as a set of actions exerted upon a territory, which in turn involves a very precise and limited degree of transformation of nature. Again, for Mansilla, Le Corbusier is not an exception here: architects like Siza or Ludwig Mies van der Rohe, both of whom started their careers working directly on stone, conceptualize their architecture as the modeling, carving, or chiseling of something that is already there. This understanding allows architects to imagine that their actions do not transform the substance of the preexisting, and therefore that nature and architecture are in essence the same thing, even if they often adopt different ways of being in the world, different attitudes or gestures.

Together with his partner Emilio Tuñón, Mansilla tested some of these ideas in the design of the Royal Collections Museum in Madrid, a building that actively challenges the categories of architecture and topography. Like many towns in central Spain, Madrid was founded on a high plateau near a river, a position that facilitated both irrigation and defense. Over the centuries, as the initial Goth hamlet was replaced by the Muslim alcazar, and later by the Royal Palace, the topology of the area was slowly architecturalized. By the time a competition was called for a museum to hold the vast collections of the Crown, in 1999, the difference in elevation between the citadel and the river had been

In his collaboration with the mathematician Edward Trouin, Le Corbursier proposed to bore through a mountain in Plan d'Aups with a series of interconnected chambers. Sketch for Basilique, La Sainte-Baume, France, 1948.

formalized as a series of retention walls. Initially intended for a site in the square between the Royal Palace and the cathedral, Mansilla and Tuñón's museum decided instead to bury itself, to literally inhabit and become the cliff between the city and the river.

The complex layering and intermingling of architecture, history, and topography present in the site was furthered during the museum's construction: as the architects dug deeper into the ground, remains of different historic settlements emerged, forcing the team to modify the design in order to incorporate them into the building, which ultimately adopted the structure of the historical and geological strata. In its final built configuration, masterfully geometricized by the architects, the museum is simultaneously a piece of infrastructure—a giant retention wall—and a series of excavated public spaces that link the upper plaza with the gardens at the level of the river. As visitors descend through the chambers of the museum, they slowly move away from the fast pace of city life, and are made aware of very different time scales of history and geology. Perhaps most importantly, and in fulfillment of the architects' ambition, the building does not replace the site, but rather becomes its latest incarnation, a mineral cornice for the city's western flank.

What makes the Royal Collections Museum different from Le Corbusier's Sainte-Baume is not just its actuality, the fact that it was built, but rather how it proactively engaged the complex and contradictory cultural, technical, and physical conditions of its making. In this project, difficult negotiations with politicians, archaeologists, engineers, and clergymen, among other stakeholders, were understood by the architects as a necessary part of the

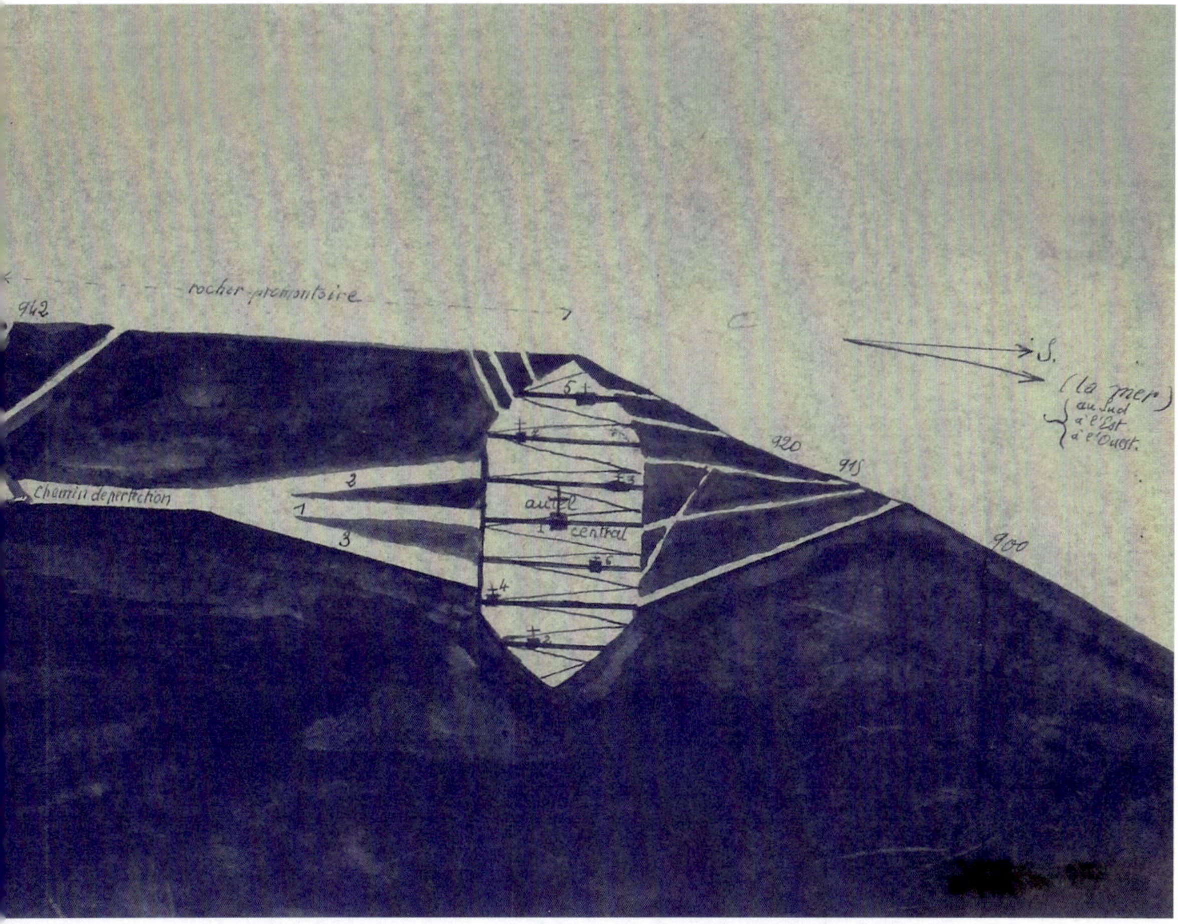

massive undertaking, and embraced as vectors that introduced additional tensions into an already violent process of displacement of vast amounts of earth and concrete.

It is important at this point to make a distinction between the subtractive approach of the Sainte-Baume, which corresponds to the extractive purism of Chillida in Tenerife, and therefore relates to a certain postwar sculptural classicism, and the more impure but involved processes of construction of the Royal Collections Museum, which in turn resonate more closely with contemporary attitudes in the field of sculpture. In Madrid, the complex negotiations and massive effort of construction of the museum project bring to mind the writings of Robert Smithson, who at the end of his career developed an understanding of land art—or earth sculpture, as he called it—as akin to mining, agriculture, and architecture, all of which he saw as processes that transform a territory through a series of concrete dialectics between nature and people and at a scale comparable to geological transformation.[3]

In his famous text "Frederick Law Olmsted and the Dialectical Landscape," Smithson discusses Central Park with a surprisingly factual and dry approach, in which the geological processes that formed its mineral substrate, the famous bedrock of Manhattan, are considered on equal terms with the displacement of tons of dirt required in the formation of its reservoirs, and even with the accumulation of garbage in the surface of the ponds due to lack of maintenance. I am not implying here that Smithson's perspective is neutral or non-judgmental, but rather that he envisions the landscape of the park as a perpetually evolving phenomenon within which human and non-human actors are continually colliding, in a process that does not necessarily elicit an immediate moral response.

Smithson's views on ecology, of which both the concrete and the quantitative are fundamental aspects, were far beyond his own time and may serve us today, not just as a lens to

Madrid's Royal Collections Museum is a stack of public spaces, voids excavated into the cliff that separates the city and river. Mansilla + Tuñón Arquitectos. Royal Collections Museum under construction, ca. 2010.

understand a project such as the Royal Collections Museum, but as a guide to reimagine the role of architecture in a new era of environmental exception, when human production and waste are the greatest force of geological transformation. Within our current context, Smithson's reflections on geology, which I find mirrored in Mansilla and Tuñón's writing and building, propel us to envision architecture through its raw materiality, as a collective endeavor deeply nested within a complex system of messy and interconnected historical and natural cycles. We could then imagine inserting ourselves in those cycles by harnessing the massive scales of contemporary global construction, generating in the process a truly geological architecture, one that would leverage its complex material dialectics to produce a radical change of course, to redefine once again the historical relationship between nature and architecture and shepherd such monumental scale of artifice toward a sustainable, even redemptive path.

The building does not replace the site, but rather becomes its latest incarnation, a mineral cornice for the city's western flank. Royal Collections Museum under construction, ca. 2010.

1 Mansilla's doctoral thesis was later published as *Apuntes de viaje al interior del tiempo* (Barcelona: Fundación Caja de Arquitectos, 2002).

2 Mansilla, 181. Author's translation.

3 Robert Smithson, "Frederick Law Olmsted and the Dialectical Landscape," *Artforum* 11, no. 6 (February 1973): 62–66.

In 1979, a group of Mexican artists realized a large-scale land art piece called the *Espacio Escultórico*. Built within the territory of the Ciudad Universitaria, the much-acclaimed campus of the Universidad Nacional Autónoma de México, it was the result of a collective effort by the artists Helen Escobedo, Manuel Felguérez, Mathias Goeritz, Hersúa, Sebastián, and Federico Silva. The work consists of sixty-four large triangular concrete volumes encircling an expressive topography of black lava-rock formations 400 feet (120 meters) in diameter. Although today the interior of the circle is striped with local flora, historical images show it as an empty and dark telluric mass. It is said that the artists used napalm—another favorite from the seventies—to eradicate all vegetation within the circle. In doing so, they transformed the existing landscape into a monochromatic texture painting:

The *Espacio Escultórico (Space of Sculpture)*: gigantic brushstrokes of solidified magma. Helen Escobedo, Manuel Felguérez, Mathias Goeritz, Hersúa, Sebastián, and Federico Silva. Ciudad Universitaria, Mexico City, 1979.

a circular tableau with gigantic brushstrokes of solidified magma. The stern geometric gesture highlighted and glorified the drama of the natural setting, the primitive forces that shaped it and that connected it with its past. But more than a celebration of a higher cosmological order, the piece can also be understood as a posthumous tribute to a cultural tour de force that shaped the architectural thinking of Mexico, a revolution that took place in the south of Mexico City and redefined the relationship between architecture and topography in a radical way.

Until the middle of the twentieth century, this austral part of Mexico City was left largely untouched. An eruption of the Xitle volcano centuries before had extended long fingers of solidified lava over the area and had turned a thriving region inhabited by the Indigenous population around Cuilcuoco into a tortuous landscape of sharp, purple-black rock. Apart from shepherds grazing their goats in the area, there had been little use of these wastelands covered with cacti, palo bobo trees, and dry shrubbery. The expanding metropolis created the need for new land to be developed, however, and it was Luis Barragán who turned his gaze toward this rugged landscape, called El Pedregal, and transformed the cultural imagery of these far-off badlands forever. In a smart effort of branding avant la lettre, he brought influential artists, such as the distinguished landscape painter and volcanologist Dr. Atl and the

Luis Barragán's Jardines del Pedregal sales pavilion: a robust architecture of thick walls and opaque volumes settled firmly in the landscape. Armando Salas Portugal, photographer. Mexico City, late 1940s.

young photographer Armando Salas Portugal, to the site; their interpretations slowly changed the general perception of this harsh, arid environment. Where most people saw uninhabitable crevices full of scorpions and snakes, Barragán envisioned a new suburban lifestyle in which geology, nature, and architecture would integrate in a new, meaningful way. As the North American scholar Keith L. Eggener writes in his wonderful book on the project, "It was for El Pedregal that Barragán first articulated the verbal rhetoric of mystery and magic, silence and serenity, sensuality and spirituality, that has been used to characterize his work ever since."[1]

In 1944, Barragán acquired a first piece of land in El Pedregal[2] and began a series of small landscape interventions to illustrate his vision. By introducing ponds, irregularly shaped lawns, and steps hewn out of volcanic stone, he shaped a more acceptable version of these rugged backlands. These "demonstration gardens" were photographed by Salas Portugal and immediately used in publicity offered to national and international media. Backed by the brothers Luis and José Alberto Bustamante, who helped acquire more land in the area, Barragán launched an extensive advertising effort that included art book–like brochures and television commercials. The media campaign was supervised and coordinated by Barragán himself, who was not only a serene, spiritual figure, but also an avid real estate developer.

For the architecture of El Pedregal, Barragán envisioned built elements that, just like the pathways, fountains, and lawns, would integrate harmoniously with the existing landscape. Illustrating this idea, he constructed a sales pavilion in 1947–48 within the area of the demonstration gardens. Similar to the Prieto House, which he started building around the same time, its composition was inspired by the earthbound character of traditional haciendas: a robust architecture of colorful thick walls and clustered opaque volumes that settled firmly into the landscape. The pavilion consisted of a low, austere volume countered by a tall square tower geometrically punctured with black holes, intended to act as dovecotes. Eggener suggests that Barragán's predilection to integrate dovecotes was not only because of their modular formal quality, but also because the birds' droppings

The demonstration gardens: "The ideal place to live." Advertisement, date unknown.

Francisco Artigas's Jardines del Pedregal sales pavilion: dynamic and transparent, with a zigzagging ramp and large windows. Roberto Luna and Fernando Luna, photographers. 1950.

would lend "an instant 'aged' patina to the setting."[3] In this sense, rootedness and history informed Barragán's work as much as modernity. His fascination with the lithograph *Pueblo Mexicano* (1930), by José Clemente Orozco, illustrates this complex coexistence well. In the lithograph, cubic architecture dances above a dramatic rocky landscape. Barragán similarly described his work at the Jardines del Pedregal as an architecture of abstract qualities, of primary geometric forms that "were intended to make [his work] distinct from but not dominant over the Pedregal landscape," as Eggener notes.[4] His sales pavilion, the Prieto House, and the "demonstration houses" he built in collaboration with Max Cetto were widely published and resonated within a global architectural scene looking for fresh takes on international-style modernism, but they hardly connected with the growing group of international industrialists and Mexican entrepreneurs who had more "modern" aspirations.

By the 1950s, there was very little construction work going on in the Pedregal development that was not directly instigated by Barragán, and the real estate venture needed a new impulse. The Bustamantes proposed the young and flamboyant architect Francisco Artigas to design and build a second sales pavilion to attract potential buyers. This new pavilion immediately struck a different tone: the building was utterly dynamic and transparent, with a zigzagging access ramp and large window frames. Supported by four small, round, black columns that dissipate in the shadows underneath the building, the whole object seemed to float magically above the volcanic rock, offering visitors panoramic views over the rugged landscape from a cantilevered terrace. This daring model of a newly arrived modern lifestyle was quickly accepted by the affluent society of postwar Mexico City, and soon Artigas became the

The dining table runs into lava-rock formations inside the Luis Bustamante house. Francisco Artigas, architect. Roberto Luna and Fernando Luna, photographers. Jardines del Pedregal, Mexico City, 1956.

most prolific architect of the Pedregal development, with more than fifty luxurious dwellings realized.

Notwithstanding its commercial success, mainstream modernist design as implemented by Artigas was frequently critiqued as a globally exported style that failed to address local conditions. Artigas's sales pavilion—and, for that matter, most of his residential work in El Pedregal—constitutes the perfect metaphor for this allegation: an imported language blithely laid on top of existing topography. In the iconic images of the Casa del Risco (1952), we see an almost collage-like superposition of two different entities, a foreign idiom unconditionally inserted into a specific and local geographic and cultural environment. Still, the awkward realization here is that the architectural outcome does not seem to sustain the accusation; one would expect that the result would a blatant mismatch, but rather, the opposite is true. The slick orthogonal lines of the modern volume establish a powerful contrast with the dark, tortuous volcanic surfaces underneath, while the sculptural rock formations are reinforced by the crisp and smooth architecture that forms its new backdrop. Both seem only to enhance one another. This powerful encounter between the existing geology and a prism-based modernism was already visible in some of the published images of Richard Neutra's Kahn House, for example. But both Barragán and Cetto, his frequent collaborator (who

Abstract geometric volumes hovering over the volcanic landscape. Francisco Artigas, architect. Roberto Luna and Fernando Luna, photographers. Casa Federico Gómez (Casa del Risco), Jardines del Pedregal, Mexico City, 1951–52.

had even worked for Neutra in San Francisco), had always been too ideologically invested in Frank Lloyd Wright's idea of "organic integration" that they failed to notice—or simply disliked—the spatial and visual qualities of absolute contrast and juxtaposition. Artigas, on the other hand, fully understood that potential. Instead of watering down an extremely popular mid-century design aesthetic by blending it into the landscape and adapting it to local materiality and building techniques, he established a strong play of binary oppositions: transparent versus opaque, natural versus industrial, smooth versus rugged, organic versus orthogonal.

Since the 1920s, architectural debate had been centered on the contrast between the abstract geometries of European modernism and the organic architecture of Frank Lloyd Wright. In the European-mechanistic ideology, the interaction between modern architecture and nature was defined by an idea of control, of antagonism. Its relationship to topography had always been one of denial, suppression, and submission: through flattening or by constructing plinths, terrains were leveled into abstract horizontal surfaces. Le Corbusier's Villa Savoie, standing so well behaved in the middle of a manicured suburban lawn, is a perfect example. In the American version defended by Wright and his followers, on the other hand, architecture sought to blend with the environment, both in terms of topography and materiality; here, Fallingwater is the iconic reference. When Artigas imported a smooth, California-inspired modernism and posed it on top of the jagged lava sea of El Pedregal, a new type of interaction between architecture and landscape emerged. It is important to clarify that many of the projects that inspired Artigas, such as the Case Study Houses, were designed as single-story steel-frame dwellings economically placed on top of a

Francisco Artigas, architect. Roberto Luna and Fernando Luna, photographers. Casa Wasung, Jardines del Pedregal, Mexico City, 1957.

horizontal foundation slab and surrounded by a neatly designed garden, even if they were set in spectacular natural landscapes. (Esther McCoy notes that "nearly all of the [Case Study Houses] were on flat pads, giving little opportunity … for a Wrightian integration into the site."[5]) Crash-landing a diaphanous prism of steel columns and horizontal slabs in a rough volcanic setting spurred an exciting new vocabulary. The dramatic topographical conditions were a perfect remedy for the looming fatigue of a modern architecture that was increasingly being flattened into a suburban lifestyle commodity. In 1944, Elizabeth Mock already suggested in the catalogue of the Museum of Modern Art exhibition *Built in USA, 1932–44* that "modern planning and site engineering make it feasible to build on rugged land … which never before had seemed usable," adding that "a site of this kind can be chosen rather than the hopelessly flat ground favored by conventional builders."[6] In many cities around the world, flat land was getting scarce or expensive, and developers and aspiring homeowners were looking for new opportunities. Adventurous architects and clients discovered that the more

A volcanic sinkhole with a swimming pool in the garden of the residence of Jose Alberto Bustamante. Francisco Artigas, architect. Roberto Luna and Fernando Luna, photographers. Jardines del Pedregal, Mexico City, 1955.

adversarial the surrounding scenery was, the more heroic the architecture looked.

Peripheral places such as Mexico City, Los Angeles, and Palm Springs played a crucial role in the revitalization of the relationship between architecture and landscape. Natural elements such as crevices, rocks, and boulders were embraced as anchor points to stage architectural fantasies and to spur new plan layouts. Around the middle of the century, topographical features became a common trope within architectural production. If not enough drama was present on the plot, large boulders were hauled to a site and decoratively scattered on lawns or around swimming pools. While the Casa das Canoas, by Oscar Niemeyer, might have been a single exception within a larger oeuvre, other architects, including Artigas, Neutra, Craig Ellwood, Albert Frey, and John Lautner, made geological presence and topographical features essential aspects of their architectural explorations.

Above and right: Advertisements for the Jardines del Pedregal printed in *Arquitectura México* (March 1955), *Artes de México* 33 (February 1961), and *Artes de México* 36 (October 1961).

S DEL PEDREGAL
ANGEL
RA VIVIR
ESES
PAGAR

JARDINES DEL PEDREGAL
DE SAN ANGEL
ORIGINALIDAD...
DISTINCION...
FELICIDAD PARA VIVIR
CIEN MESES
PARA PAGAR
INFORMES Y VENTAS EN PASEO DEL PEDREGAL: TEL. 48-31-15
Y EN NUESTRAS OFICINAS GENERALES DE INSURGENTES 453 1er. PISO TEL. 11-99-40

1 Keith L. Eggener, *Luis Barragán's Gardens of El Pedregal* (New York: Princeton Architectural Press, 2001), 2.
2 Emilio Ambasz, *The Architecture of Luis Barragán* (New York: Museum of Modern Art, 1976), 11.
3 Eggener, 39.
4 Eggener, 49.
5 Esther McCoy, "Arts & Architecture Case Study Houses," in *Blueprints for Modern Living*, ed. Elizabeth A. T. Smith (Cambridge, MA: MIT Press, 1989), 37.
6 Elizabeth Mock, *Built in USA, 1932–44* (New York: Museum of Modern Art, 1944), 23.

ELEVATED SURFACE DEPRESSED

Carlos Bedoya

In 1967, following a short stay in New York City, the American artist Michael Heizer undertook a series of journeys across the United States. Fascinated by the beauty of the landscapes, the immense objects (such as rocks) he encountered, and the vast absence of the plains, he began to experiment with a series of projects that would maintain a fundamental relationship with natural elements, whether through their presence or their absence. As he explained in a 1984 interview, "I was interested in massive objects as well as the absence of objects."[1]

In some of these projects, he used large rocks as natural sculptures that he relocated, transplanted, and displaced with the idea of imposing or creating new conditions of meaning. In *Elevated Surface Depressed* (1982), three enormous rocks were placed on plinths that elevated one rock, left

***Elevated Surface Depressed*: three enormous rocks placed on plinths that elevate one rock, leave another at ground level, and drop the third below grade. Michael Heizer. 1982.**

another at ground level, and dropped the third below ground level. This exercise enabled reflection on the differences between the natural objects—the rocks—and between their new positions on the various bases. It also generated a contrast between the irregular geometries of the natural elements and the orthogonal angles of the plinths.

Another example is *Double Negative*, a work developed between 1969 and 1970 at Mormon Mesa, in Nevada, in which Heizer removed rock from two mesas that faced each other across a natural void, creating another void. The French poet and critic Jacques Dupin wrote, "The void is not nothing, but rather the matrix of space. It is only defined by what it excludes or ignores."[2] Similarly, Claude Debussy defined the void as a charged potential between two sounds.[3] *Double Negative* generates a tension between the excavated spaces by visually linking the voids along a single axis; this alignment meant that the intervention appeared to grow until its size could be compared to that of the Empire State Building. Although architecture does not operate with the same tools as art, the possibilities offered by the physical relationship between architecture and the line of the terrain on which it is erected—its location on a site—are clear. These possibilities prompt different reflections and questions involving urban, social, and political spheres.

How architecture is set in its context has long been one of the leading concerns of the profession. In his 1485 treatise *De re aedificatoria*, Leon Battista Alberti writes, "All the intent and purpose of lineaments lies in finding the correct, infallible way of joining and fitting together those lines and angles which define and enclose the surfaces of a building. It is the function and duty of lineaments, then, to prescribe an appropriate place, exact numbers, a proper scale, and a graceful order for whole buildings and for each of their constituent parts, so that the whole form and appearance of the building may depend on the lineaments alone."[4] For Alberti, topography—"an appropriate place," "a proper scale"—is a crucial consideration in the process of design.

Since well before Alberti, engagement with the terrain has yielded intelligent architectural solutions. At Lalibela, a religious complex built in Ethiopia during the twelfth and thirteenth centuries, each building is carved out below ground level, a technique that facilitated the construction of complex, high-ceilinged spaces. In an Indian stepwell, systems of staircases functionally and visually define the interior of a below-ground water basin, giving access to different levels of the void in accordance with shifting water levels throughout the year. In the archeological zone of Paquimé, in Chihuahua, Mexico, twelfth-century

In *Double Negative*, Michael Heizer removed 240,000 tons of rock from two mesas facing each other across a natural void. Mormon Mesa, Overton, Nevada, 1969.

Heizer's *Displaced/Replaced Mass* relocates rocks into rectangular openings in a gallery floor. 1994.

inhabitants built partially subterranean constructions with thick adobe walls that helped maintain a comfortable temperature year-round, thanks to the thermal mass of the soil.

Later, in the modernist period, architects sought the partial or complete separation of the building from the ground for a variety of reasons. In 1962, Clorindo Testa designed the National Library in Buenos Aires, a building located on a large site along one of the city's most prestigious avenues, close to the Rio de la Plata. Testa's scheme disposes the building in three positions relative to

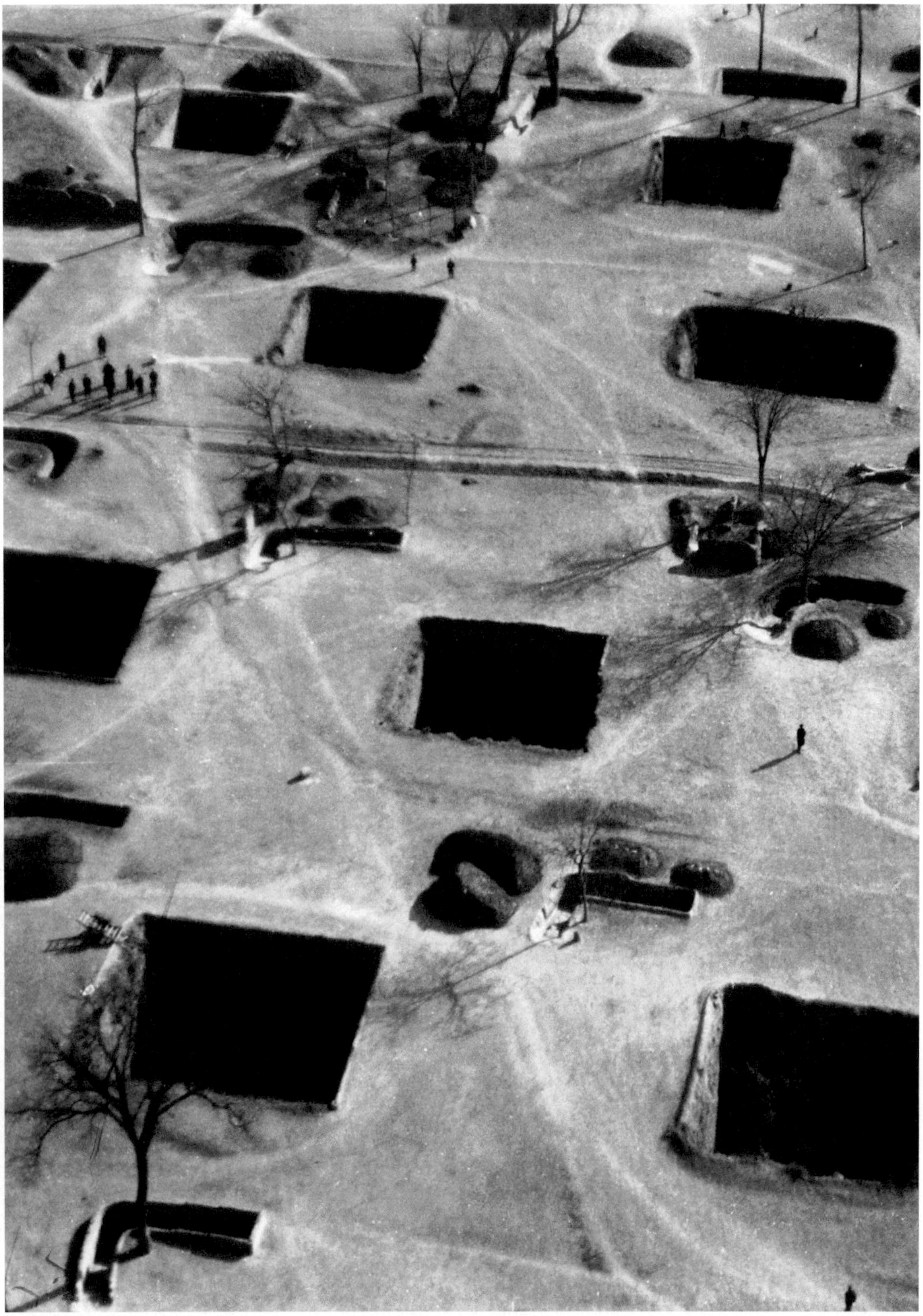

From a plane, underground courtyards allowing natural ventilation and daylight appear as black perforations. Underground village near Tunkwan, China, date unknown. Photograph by Wulf-Diether Graf zu Castell-Rüdenhausen, 1930s.

the horizontal of the terrain. To one side, one of the project's major volumes, the book depository, is buried. At street level, the building frees up as much room as possible, increasing the available public space by suspending the principal volume on four huge hollow columns containing staircases and elevators. This gesture also makes it possible to cover part of the plaza. The raised volume contains all the reading rooms, exhibition galleries, administrative offices, cafeteria, terraces, and so on, which enjoy unbroken views toward the Rio de la Plata thanks to their position above the street.

Ludwig Mies van der Rohe pursued a similar strategy in response to a different problem in 1945, when he was commissioned by Edith Farnsworth to design a country house in Plano, Illinois, on a site adjacent to the Fox River. Mies decided to raise the house using a lightweight, white-painted metal structure in such a way that the horizontal floor and ceiling slabs not only appear as limpid, pristine elements in relation to the irregular site, but also create an impression that the home is subtly floating above the surface of the terrain. The move also provided a secondary benefit: raising the house helped prevent potential flooding when the river overflows. In 1971, a subsequent occupant of the Farnsworth House, Peter Palumbo, the owner of a large building firm, commissioned the architects Peter Carter and Adrian Gale to construct a small boathouse on the riverbank. They

A system of staircases functionally and visually defines the interior of a below-ground water basin. Chand Baori stepwell, Abhaneri, Rajasthan, India, eighth to eighteenth century CE.

employed a totally different strategy to that used by Mies in the house itself, designing an open structure with a pitched wooden roof, supported by low concrete walls that serve to contain the water and earth.

Exemplary cases such as these, which reflect on this essential, basic relationship between an object or a building and the horizontal line generated by topography, help us to begin to understand the potential that exists in the interaction of these two elements. The simple act of determining the position of a building in relation to its site is a powerful one, with the

The Lalibela churches of Ethiopia were hewn out of monolithic rock formations. Church of Saint George, late twelfth to early thirteenth century CE.

potential to give rise to multiple possibilities and readings. What happens if a building is buried? Or if it is raised above ground level? What happens if its footprint is minimal, or if it occupies the maximum area of the site? What does a large single volume do that a series of buildings does not, and vice versa? And how might these questions inform the mechanisms with which we operate as architects in the contemporary city?

The Farnsworth House boathouse—with its pitched roof, traditional materials, and decorative medallion—appears as the antithesis of a Miesian floating box. Peter Carter and Adrian Gale. Plano, Illinois, 1971.

The elevated volume of the Museu de Arte de São Paulo creates a covered plaza at ground level. Lina Bo Bardi. 1968.

Hans Hollein's proposed Museum in the Rock is fully enclosed by Salzburg's Mönchsberg formation. It has no visible facade. Section model, 1989–2002.

1 Michael Heizer, interview by Julia Brown, in *Michael Heizer: Sculpture in Reverse*, ed. Julia Brown (Los Angeles: Museum of Contemporary Art, Los Angeles, 1984), 8.
2 Jacques Dupin quoted in Sol Madridejos and Juan Carlos Sancho Osinaga, "La paradoja del vacio," *CIRCO* 6 (1993): 6. Author's translation.
3 See Madridejos and Sancho Osinaga. Both Debussy's and Dubin's categorizations of the void figure into Madrilejos and Sancho Osinaga's argument.
4 Leon Battista Alberti, *De re aedificatoria*, trans. Joseph Rykwert et al. (1485; Cambridge, MA: MIT Press, 1988), 7.

Carlos Bedoya is an architect based in Mexico City and a principal of PRODUCTORA, a firm he co-founded in 2006 with Wonne Ickx, Victor Jaime, and Abel Perles. He studied architecture at the Universidad Iberoamericana, in Mexico City, and received a master's degree in criticism and design from the Escuela Técnica Superior de Arquitectura de Barcelona. Before forming PRODUCTORA, he worked at Josep Maria Botey and Flores & Prats Studio in Barcelona, and with Enrique Norten and Fernando Romero as a project director in Mexico City. Bedoya has lectured about PRODUCTORA's work worldwide and has written about architecture in different media. He has taught at TEC de Monterrey, the Universidad Iberoamericana, and Illinois Institute of Technology, and has led workshops in the United States and South America. He is a founding partner of LIGA - Space for Architecture - Mexico City, an independent platform that, since 2011, has stimulated an interchange of ideas and investigation on contemporary Latin American architecture. He has also been a member of the editorial board of *Domus Mexico*.

Frank Escher, trained at the ETH in Zurich, is a principal of the Los Angeles–based practice Escher GuneWardena Architecture. A monograph, *Clocks and Clouds: The Architecture of Escher GuneWardena*, was published by Birkhäuser in 2017. Escher is the editor of *John Lautner, Architect* (Artemis, 1994), the first monograph on Lautner's work; oversaw the John Lautner Archive from 1995 to 2007, when it was acquired by the Getty Research Institute; and is a co-author, with Jean-Louis Cohen and Nicholas Olsberg, of *Between Earth and Heaven: The Architecture of John Lautner* (Rizzoli, 2007). Escher serves on the board of the John Lautner Foundation, is an advisor to the Julius Shulman Institute, and is a past board member and president and now an advisor of the Los Angeles Forum for Architecture and Urban Design. Escher has taught at the University of Southern California and, jointly with Ravi GuneWardena, at the University of Oregon and the École polytechnique fédérale de Lausanne.

Wonne Ickx studied civil engineering and architecture at the University of Ghent, in Belgium, and the Escuela Técnica Superior de Arquitectura de Madrid. He continued his education with a master's degree in urban studies from the Centre for Metropolitan Studies (CEMET) at the University of Guadalajara, Mexico. He worked for several years as a project director at Neutelings Riedijk in Rotterdam and at Fernando Romero in Mexico City. In 2006, he founded PRODUCTORA in Mexico City, together with Carlos Bedoya, Victor Jaime, and Abel Perles. Ickx has taught architecture and urbanism at the Universidad Iberoamericana, the Universidad La Salle, and the Centro de Diseño in Mexico City and at the University of California, Los Angeles. He has lectured worldwide about his work. He is founding director of LIGA - Space for Architecture - Mexico City, an independent platform that , since 2011, has stimulated an interchange of ideas and investigation on contemporary Latin American architecture. He has been part of the editorial board of *Arquine* since 2010.

Véronique Patteeuw is an architect, writer, and editor based in Brussels. She is an associate professor at the École nationale supérieure d'architecture et du paysage Lille and editor of *OASE*. Her research focuses on the theory and history of architectural representation in relation to the history of the postmodern. Her PhD research, "Architects without Architecture," dealt with the potential of architectural periodicals at the École des Beaux-Arts in Paris as a radical alternative to architectural pedagogy at that time. Together with Léa-Catherine Szacka, she published the book *Mediated Messages* (Bloomsbury, 2017), an edited volume on the role of magazines and exhibitions in the creation of a postmodern architecture. Patteeuw regularly writes in architectural journals and has lectured at the École polytechnique fédérale de Lausanne, Columbia University, the École nationale supérieure d'architecture de Versailles, the University of Ghent, and the University of Manchester.

Jesús Vassallo is a Spanish architect and writer based in Houston and Madrid. His work interrogates the problem of realism in architecture through the production of design projects and scholarship. Vassallo studied architecture at Harvard University's Graduate School of Design (MArch II) and the Escuela Técnica Superior de Arquitectura de Madrid (PhD). He is the author of *Seamless: Digital Collage and Dirty Realism in Contemporary Architecture* (Park Books, 2016). His articles have been published internationally in magazines such as *AA Files, 2G, Log, Harvard Design Magazine, Future Anterior, Domus, and Arquitectura Viva*. Since 2011, he has also been an editor of *CIRCO* magazine. In 2012, Vassallo became an assistant professor at the Rice School of Architecture, and in 2015, he founded an independent design practice that bridges architecture and urbanism through an understanding of both as material culture.

77 ON TOPOGRAPHY: PRODUCTORA AT S. R. CROWN HALL – PROJECTS 2006–17
On November 9, 2018, PRODUCTORA and the Illinois Institute of Technology (IIT) College of Architecture hosted a symposium that examined the relationship between buildings and the ground they occupy, followed by the opening of an exhibition of our projects read through the idea of architecture as a constructed ground. The symposium functioned as a kind of public workshop for the book's authors, who reflected on several moments in architectural history in conversation with IIT faculty. The images that follow re-present those in the exhibition, which were selected retroactively for their ability to illustrate our interest in natural topography as an elementary force that encourages PRODUCTORA's architectural proposals.

TEOTITLÁN DEL VALLE COMMUNITY CULTURAL CENTER, OAXACA, MEXICO, 2016
The large covered staircase of the museum connects the main square of the small Indigenous village with the river below. It hereby inserts itself in a sequence of existing public spaces positioned along the topography of the town.

BLAS HOUSE, VALLE DE BRAVO, MEXICO, 2013
Instead of terracing the steep plot parallel to the topography lines, a horizontal square is inserted over a 45 degree angle, creating very different spatial conditions on either side: one of the corners protrudes far out over the existing landscape, while the opposite corner is tucked away deep into the ground.

CASA DIAZ, VALLE DE BRAVO, MEXICO, 2011
To maximize lake views, the building takes the form of long rectangular prisms, each with one side completely open to the lake. Following the natural slope, these volumes are dynamically stacked to allow each to give access to a terrace placed on top of the volume below.

MUSEO DE ARTE CONTEMPORÁNEO LIMAC, PERU, 2006
The LiMAC museum has no facade or silhouette. It is a buried space illuminated through patios and skylights. The museum manifests itself as a series of square excavations and triangular volumes in the landscape: an abstract composition, like a Nazca drawing, in the Peruvian desert.

TEOPANZOLCO CULTURAL CENTER, CUERNAVACA, MEXICO, 2017
A stepped triangular esplanade forms the roof of the auditorium. This inclined surface supports the smaller triangular roof of the main lobby. Both platforms descend in opposite directions and create a visual interplay of inclined planes in a direct dialogue with the existing landscape and the adjacent pre-Hispanic pyramids.

HOUSE IN TEQUESQUITENGO, MORELOS, MEXICO, 2013
The project remodels an existing weekend house. By leveling an outdoor platform halfway between the lower floor and the upper floor of the residence, an existing staircase and guamúchil tree and a new swimming pool become the lead actors of the reconfigured spatial composition.

HOUSE IN GINIGALA, SRI LANKA, 2012

The lower floor of this residence is a concrete structure terraced according to the existing topography. The roof of that same space is a perfectly horizontal slab, creating a variety of interior heights. The upper level is made of palm wood and placed on top of the horizontal datum.

MALI MUSEUM EXPANSION, PERU, 2016

The main gesture of this museum extension is the excavation of a deep rectangular patio next to the historic building. The void has an interior facade that mimics the order and proportion of the neoclassical elevation, establishing a dialogue between the existing building and the addition.

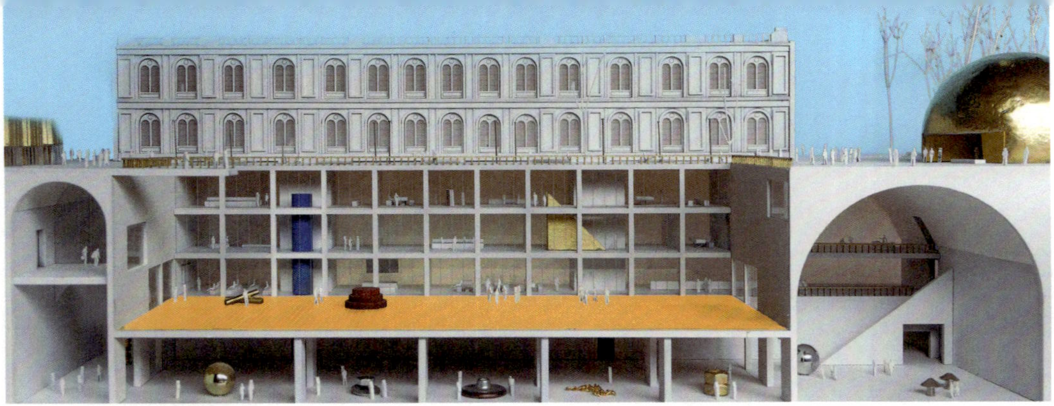

TSUNAMI MEMORIAL SITE, OSLO, 2006
By inserting a perfect square into the site—trapped in between the condition of sea and land—we provide a spatial experience around (and in) a constantly changing piece of nature. Situating the Platonic form in between low and high sea level, the square can become an extension of land toward the sea, or can be taken by the sea and almost disappear.

HOUSE IN CHIHUAHUA, CHIHUAHUA, MEXICO, 2008
This residential project is excavated into the slope of the hill, reducing its exterior appearance almost completely to the roof surface: a triangulated facade that follows the contours of the surrounding landscape.

FLEISCHMANN RESIDENCE, LOS ANGELES, 2017
This house in the Echo Park neighborhood of Los Angeles was amplified by excavating underneath an existing 1920s tract house. Toward the back of the house, a new steel moment frame was added to intensify the relationship between the interior space, the garden, and the horizon.

AALTO UNIVERSITY CAMPUS COMPETITION, ESPOO, FINLAND, 2012
This competition entry for a new School of Arts, Design and Architecture uses a large circular cutout in the earth to group a series of buildings into a single ensemble. The volumes are connected by interior circulation on the first below-ground level.

PRODUCTORA

PRODUCTORA is a Mexico City–based architectural studio founded in 2006 by Carlos Bedoya (1973, Mexico), Wonne Ickx (1974, Belgium), Victor Jaime (1978, Mexico), and Abel Perles (1972, Argentina). The studio's work is distinguished by an interest in precise geometries, the production of clearly legible projects with limited gestures, and the search for timeless buildings.

PRODUCTORA has been recognized by the Architectural League of New York with the Young Architects Forum (2007) and Emerging Voices (2013) awards. In 2016, they received the Mies Crown Hall Americas Prize for Emerging Practice from Illinois Institute of Technology in Chicago for the Pavilion on the Zocalo. In 2018, PRODUCTORA was recognized with the Oscar Niemeyer Award for Latin American Architecture for the Teopanzolco Cultural Center, a project realized in collaboration with Isaac Broid. That same project also received the Simon Architecture Prize - Living Places in Barcelona, a recognition organized in collaboration with the Fundació Mies van der Rohe that celebrates collective places in which public and community life develops.

The partners of PRODUCTORA have taught at local institutions such as the Universidad Iberoamericana, the Centro de Diseño, TEC de Monterrey, and the Universidad La Salle in Mexico City as well as international universities such as the University of California, Los Angeles, Illinois Institute of Technology, and Harvard University's Graduate School of Design.

In 2011, PRODUCTORA founded, alongside curator and art critic Ruth Estévez, LIGA - Space for Architecture - Mexico City, a platform that promotes emerging Latin American architecture through exhibitions, conferences, and workshops. www.liga-df.com

Image credits

Images spanning multiple pages are listed by the first page on which they appear.

page 11 Courtesy Estate of Marvin Rand
pages 12 and 13 © F.L.C. / ADAGP, Paris / Artists Rights Society (ARS), New York 2020
page 14 left Courtesy Pelli Clarke Pelli Architects
pages 14 right and 15 Courtesy Proyecto Helicoide (www.proyectohelicoide.com)
page 16 Courtesy Safdie Architects
page 17 Photograph by Soichi Sunami. © 2020 The Isamu Noguchi Foundation and Garden Museum, New York / Artists Rights Society (ARS), New York
page 19 Image courtesy Wonne Ickx. Fair use
page 20 left Courtesy Legorreta
pages 20 right and 21 Images courtesy Wonne Ickx. Fair use
pages 22–25 Courtesy Legorreta
page 27 Photograph by Aris Konstantinidis. Courtesy Dimitri Konstantinidis and Alexandra Tsoukala
page 28 left Courtesy Yale School of Architecture
page 28 right Photograph by Aris Konstantinidis. Courtesy Dimitri Konstantinidis and Alexandra Tsoukala
pages 29 and 30 left © Hélène Binet
pages 30 right and 32–34 Photographs by Nicolò Galeazzi. Courtesy atelier XYZ
page 37 R. M. Schindler papers, Architecture and Design Collection. Art, Design & Architecture Museum, UC, Santa Barbara
page 38 Courtesy Frank Escher
pages 39–40 John Lautner papers, Getty Research Institute, Los Angeles (2007.M.13). © Heirs or estate of Leland Y. Lee, with permission of The John Lautner Foundation
page 41 John Lautner papers, Getty Research Institute, Los Angeles (2007.M.13). © 2020 The John Lautner Foundation
pages 42–43 John Lautner papers, Getty Research Institute, Los Angeles (2007.M.13). © Heirs or estate of Leland Y. Lee, with permission of The John Lautner Foundation
page 44 Getty Research Institute, Los Angeles (2004.R.10). © J. Paul Getty Trust
page 47 Médiathèque de l'Architecture et du Patrimoine, Charenton-le-Pont, France. © Ministère de la Culture / Médiathèque du Patrimoine, Dist. RMN-Grand Palais / Art Resource, NY
page 48 Inv. 80.2.27. Don Georges Hilbert, 1980. © Ville de Versailles, Musée Lambinet
page 49 Photograph by Daniel Díaz Font. Courtesy Estate of Eduardo Chillida and Hauser & Wirth. © Zabalaga-Leku, Artists Rights Society (ARS), New York 2020
page 50 © F.L.C. / ADAGP, Paris / Artists Rights Society (ARS), New York 2020
page 52 Courtesy Luis Asín
page 55 Printed in *PROCESS* 39, “Modern Mexican Architecture” (1983): 76. Fair use
page 56 left © 2020 Barragan Foundation, Switzerland / Artists Rights Society (ARS), New York
page 56 right Photograph by Armando Salas Portugal. © 2020 Barragan Foundation, Switzerland / Artists Rights Society (ARS), New York
pages 57–60 Courtesy Archive Roberto Luna and Fernando Luna
pages 62–63 Images courtesy Hemeroteca Nacional UNAM. Fair use
page 65 Photograph by Peter Harholdt. Image courtesy Collection Martin Z. Margulies, Miami. © Michael Heizer
page 66 left Photograph by John Weber. Collection: Museum of Contemporary Art, Los Angeles. © Michael Heizer
page 66 right Inhotim Collection, Brazil. © Michael Heizer
page 67 Deutsches Museum, Munich, Archives, CD_69995
page 68 left Photograph by Doron. CC BY-SA 3.0
page 68 right © Michael Poliza
page 70 left Courtesy Anita Pedersen Warren
page 70 right CC0 1.0 Universal Public Domain
page 71 © Private Archive Hollein
page 77 Courtesy Carlos Bedoya
pages 78–96 © PRODUCTORA. All images by PRODUCTORA except:
pages 78–82 Luis Gallardo
pages 84 right and 85 Paul Czitrom
pages 86 right and 87–91 Luis Gallardo
page 94 Iwan Baan
page 95 Rory Gardiner

Cover photograph by Luis Gallardo. © PRODUCTORA

Endpaper captions and credits, from front to back of book:

Albert Frey, architect. Julius Shulman, photographer. Frey House, Palm Springs, California, 1964. Getty Research Institute, Los Angeles (2004.R.10). © J. Paul Getty Trust

Richard Neutra, architect. Julius Shulman, photographer. Stone-Fisher Platform Houses, Los Angeles, 1965. Getty Research Institute, Los Angeles (2004.R.10). © J. Paul Getty Trust

Tita Carloni, architect. Casa Balmelli, Rovio, Switzerland, 1956. Courtesy Fondazione Archivi Architetti Ticinesi

Richard Neutra, architect. Julius Shulman, photographer. Stone-Fisher Platform Houses, Los Angeles, 1965. Getty Research Institute, Los Angeles (2004.R.10). © J. Paul Getty Trust

Albert Frey, architect. Julius Shulman, photographer. Frey House, Palm Springs, California, 1964. Getty Research Institute, Los Angeles (2004.R.10). © J. Paul Getty Trust

Craig Ellwood, architect. Julius Shulman, photographer. Zack House, Los Angeles, 1952. Getty Research Institute, Los Angeles (2004.R.10). © J. Paul Getty Trust

H. U. Scherer, project architect. Metron Architektengruppe, execution. Mühlehalde Terrace Housing, Umiken, Switzerland, 1963–71. Courtesy Metron

Craig Ellwood, architect. ArtCenter College of Design Hillside campus, ca. 1977 (2004.26.309). © ArtCenter College of Design, Pasadena, CA

Colophon

Concept: PRODUCTORA (Carlos Bedoya, Wonne Ickx, Victor Jaime, Abel Perles)
Contributors: Carlos Bedoya, Frank Escher, Wonne Ickx, Véronique Patteeuw, Jesús Vassallo
Design: Mainstudio (Edwin van Gelder, Florian Schimanski)
Coordination: Tessa Watson, Jayne Kelley
Copyediting and text supervision: Jayne Kelley
Image supervision: Jayne Kelley, Tessa Watson
Printing and lithography: robstolk

PRODUCTORA would like to thank IIT and the College of Architecture, especially Wiel Arets, Dirk Denison, and Sasha Zanko; Michelangelo Sabatino, Lluís Ortega, Andrew Jiang, and all IIT faculty, students, and staff who contributed to the exhibition and symposium in S. R. Crown Hall on November 9, 2018; and Sarah Herda and the Graham Foundation for Advanced Studies in the Fine Arts for hosting a conversation between the contributors of this book in the afternoon before the symposium.

We are very grateful to everyone that helped us locate and granted us permission to use the many images in this book. Special thanks go to Dolores Robles at Legorreta, Antti Rüegg at Metron / ETH, the family of Roberto y Fernando Luna, and the librarians at the Arts Library at UCLA.

Finally, we would like to thank those who formed part of our studios at IIT and were crucial sparring partners in developing the ideas represented in this book: in the "Being the Mountain" studio, our co-instructor Agata Siemionow and students Edgar Alvarado, Luke Downen, Daniel Godziszewski, Zhitao Hu, Karam Lee, Jennifer Nakano, Neesha Narayanan, Andi Piper, Leslie Schamber, Daniela Sesma Espinoza, Katsia Seviarynchyk, Marta Wojcik, Cristian Yugsi, and Ernesto Zuniga; and in the "Elevated Surface Depressed" studio, our co-instructor Joseph Altschuler and students Kat Bernardo, Kurt Cheang, Ling Deng, Maria Escario, Isabel Fitzpatrick-Meyer, Piotr Jelonek, Marcus Malesh, Christina Mikhail, Jess Monigal, Paul Nagtalon, Alessandro Signori, Daniel Tangaro, Alejandro Valencia, and Elizabeth Vasquez.

MCHAP
This publication and the Mies Crown Hall Americas Prize (MCHAP) are initiatives of Illinois Institute of Technology's College of Architecture.

MCHAP would like to thank all those who made this program and publication possible: IIT, the College of Architecture and the Lambert Fund, the City of Chicago, and the firms, institutions, and individuals that generously support the initiative, including the Canadian Centre for Architecture, the Alphawood Foundation, Kohler, and the Mies van der Rohe Society at Illinois Institute of Technology.

Illinois Institute of Technology
Reed Kroloff, Dean, IIT College of Architecture
Dirk Denison, Director, MCHAP
Sasha Zanko, MCHAP Program Coordinator

Published by:

IITAC Press
IIT College of Architecture
3360 South State Street
Chicago, IL 60616-3793
USA
www.arch.iit.edu

Actar Publishers
New York Barcelona
www.actar.com

Distributed by:

Actar D, Inc.

New York
440 Park Avenue South, 17th Floor
New York, NY 10016
USA
+1 2129662207
salesnewyork@actar-d.com

Barcelona
Roca i Batlle, 2-4
08023 Barcelona, Spain
+34 933 282 183
eurosales@actar-d.com

Printed in the Netherlands
ISBN: 9781948765510
LCCN: 2020932411
A CIP catalogue record for this book is available from the Library of Congress, Washington, DC, USA